A Remarkable Journey

*A TIMELINE OF REV. SUN MYUNG MOON,
DR. HAK JA HAN MOON,
AND THE UNIFICATION CHURCH*

Introduction

The story of Rev. Sun Myung Moon and Dr. Hak Ja Han Moon is a remarkable journey. From the humblest beginnings in occupied Korea, through the war-ravaged countryside of the Korean War, from persecution at home and misunderstanding on a global level, this couple have stood fast to their single-minded vision—to become the True Parents this world so desperately needs.

This book began as the material in a timeline display at East Garden, NY., the home base of Rev. and Dr. Moon during their activities in the United States, where they focused their ministry for over 40 years. Tours of the East Garden Estate culminate with this display. In many ways the book outlines the trail of hardship and tears they have been through. It also takes into account the steadfast resolve they have shown to care for the people of the world.

They have founded countless humanitarian and research organizations, foundations to further the cause of peace and the arts, and have continued through all these years to stress their utmost commitment to the institution of marriage between men and women as the bedrock of global peace. When peace begins in the family, it organically spreads to the community, nation and world. They have called on every single person to heed this call to recognize their own God-given uniqueness and therefore understand their own role, no matter how small or large, in seeing the establishment of Kingdom of Heaven on earth.

1920
SUN MYUNG MOON

Birthplace in North Korea

On January 6, 1920 (lunar date), Sun Myung Moon is born into a family of farmers in Sangsa-ri, North Pyeongan Province, now part of North Korea. *(The photo shows a reconstruction of the house. Below is Rev. Moon's drawing of his childhood home.)*

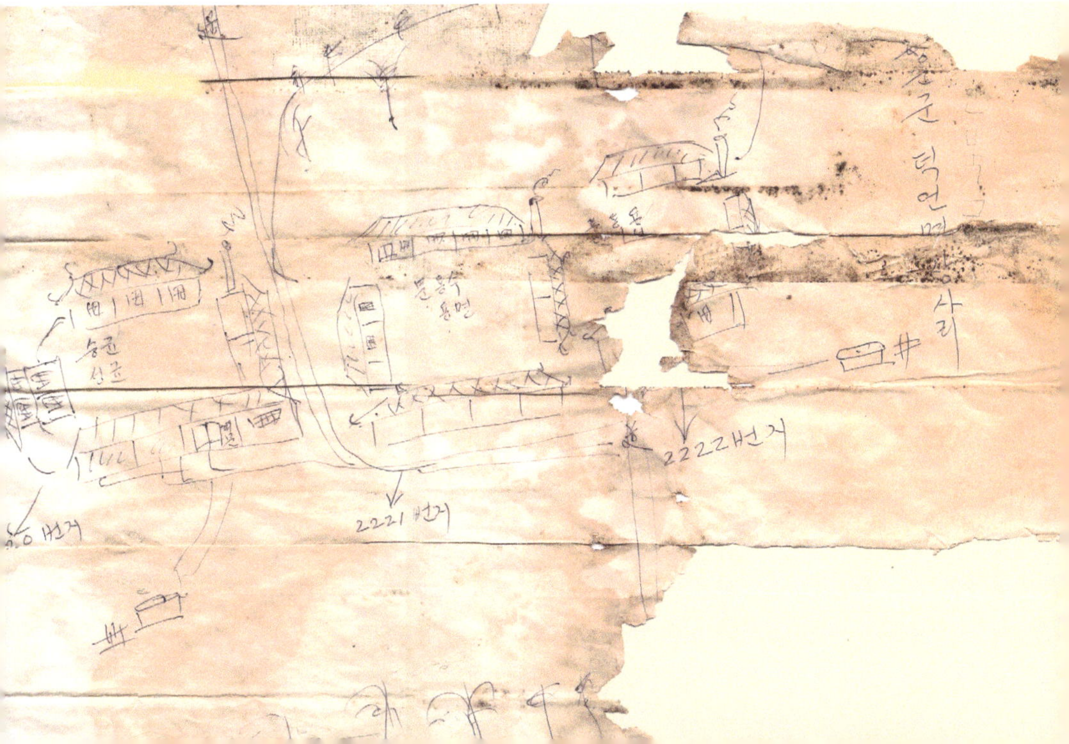

The Young Sun Myung Moon

As a boy Sun Myung Moon (bottom row, directly under the writing on the building) studies at a Confucian school and is a keen observer of the natural world. Around 1930, his parents become fervent Christians and the young Sun Myung Moon becomes a Sunday school teacher.

From the age of 7 to 13 True Father studies at the village Confucian school. There he learns Chinese characters and reads the Confucian classics. His memory is excellent, and his calligraphy is superb. At this time, his dream is to acquire three doctoral degrees so he enrolls at the Won-bong Preparatory School, then in 1934 he enters Osan Primary School and in April 1935, he transfers to the Jeongju Public Primary School, mainly to study Japanese.

On March 25, 1938, at his graduation ceremony, he volunteers to speak at the podium. He gives a long speech to express his views; one by one he points out the wrongs of Japanese colonial educational policy and its hypocrisy. Because of this incident, the Japanese police add his name to their list as a person to be watched.

Japan occupies and rules Korea at this time. Growing up oppressed in his own land, Sun Myung Moon learns the pain of injustice at the hands of the Japanese rulers.

Traits I Inherited from My Family

"I resemble my mother in many ways; I have my mother's revolutionary disposition and I inherited my creativity from my mother.

My father, on the other hand, was more like a scholar. Once he heard something he never forgot it, like today's computers. He had a photographic memory.

My maternal grandfather was also this way; he was innovative. In his village, he was involved in ocean-related work, and he was quite creative about it. So when I was six, seven and eight years old I used to visit him at his home and follow him around catching fish. You have no idea how excited I was, and how anxiously I waited for an opportunity to go and see him."

If a beggar came to our home asking for food, my grandfather *(photo above)* would pick up his meal and take it to that beggar. Perhaps because I was born into such a family, I too have spent much of my life feeding people. To me, giving people food is the most precious work. When I am eating and I see someone who has nothing to eat, it pains my heart and I cannot continue eating."

—Rev. Sun Myung Moon

My Life As a Student

"In the village school that taught Chinese characters, classics and calligraphy, there were people from age nine up into their twenties and thirties. ... We practiced writing Chinese characters every day. The teacher used the characters I wrote as models for other students to follow and copy. This was before I was even 12.

After studying at the village school, I joined a small private school that specialized in teaching art. I am a really talented artist. There for the first time in my life I learned how to draw and paint pictures. For my first picture, I contemplated what flowers I was going to draw. Looking at the size of the paper, I calculated their sizes and locations in my head. With this plan in mind I made a rough sketch of the flowers; next, I completed the coloring, and there it was, my first picture. They hung that drawing on the wall at the school.

When I studied, I studied like lightning. In no time I finished materials that would take years for an ordinary person. My hometown is a small farming village located eight kilometers northeast of Jeongju. It seems like just yesterday that I was studying there, at night under a kerosene lamp. I made friends with the insects that came out at night. Especially in summer, as I sat still and studied until 2:00 or 3:00 in the morning. Nighttime in the countryside is very tranquil. The sounds of the insects on such moonlit nights are simply mesmerizing."

—Rev. Sun Myung Moon

What I Learned From Nature

Rev. Moon often shared stories and lessons from his youth, showing how God used nature and the people in his life to teach him universal truths of love.

"The reason I love the forest is because all the peace in the world dwells there. Life forms in the forest do not fight each other. Of course, they eat one another and are eaten, but that is because they are hungry and need to sustain themselves. They do not fight out of enmity.

Birds do not hate other birds. Animals do not hate other animals. Trees do not hate other trees. There needs to be an absence of enmity for peace to come. Human beings are the only ones who hate other members of the same species. People hate other people because their country is different, their religion is different, and their way of thinking is different."

—Rev. Sun Myung Moon

Studying in Seoul

After graduating from Jeongju Public Primary School, Sun Myung Moon goes to Seoul.

From April 12, 1938 to March 8, 1941 he attends the Gyeongseong School of Commerce and Industry, located in Heukseok-dong. He makes sure he is always the first to arrive at school in the morning, and he often takes responsibility to clean his classroom by himself. Because he is so exemplary, his classmates afforded him respect. He protects the weak and does not hesitate to confront arrogant and strong bullies in order to teach them right from wrong.

Although he has an active personality, Sun Myung Moon rarely speaks, being serious and sincere. In order to find the way to heaven and cultivate his character, he is silent much of the time. His report card records that he is "cheerful, active, sincere and serious, strong, healthy-minded, volunteers to do things, and hard-working." It further states, "He is physically fit and strong, ass a good attendance record, and likes soccer."

Also In This Decade

1920 Mahatma Gandhi founds the non-violent liberation movement Satyagraha in India
1924 Lenin dies and Joseph Stalin seizes power in the Soviet Union
1927 The first talking movie is "The Jazz Singer"
1928 September 28: Discovery of Penicillin
1929 October: Wall Street crash

1930
JESUS AND THE DIVINE PRINCIPLE

Meeting Jesus in the Korean Mountains

Easter Sunday, 1935 (Painting by S. Watanabe) A young Sun Myung Moon accepts his mission and seeks to understand God's plan.

Troubled by the immense gap between religious ideals and the actual state of the world, he begins his own ardent pursuit of solutions through a life of prayer and study.

Early Easter morning 1935, Jesus appears to a sixteen year old Sun Myung Moon as he prays in the Korean mountains. In that vision, Jesus asks him to continue the work that he began nearly 2,000 years earlier and complete the task of establishing God's kingdom on earth bringing peace to humankind. The young Korean is stunned. After deep reflection, meditation and prayer, he pledges to take on this overwhelming mission and immediately sets out to understand its full meaning; in asking him to complete Jesus' mission, is Jesus saying there was more he was meant to complete?

Is salvation through the cross all that humankind needs or is there something more? What is it that Jesus left undone?

If sin is not completely solved, then what is the actual root of sin? What is God's plan for all the world's religions?

Jesus' Messages Open a New World

"On those days when my prayers and dedication connected to Heaven, Jesus appeared to me without fail and conveyed special messages.

If I were earnest in my desire to know something, Jesus would appear with a gentle expression and give me answers of truth. His words were always on the mark, and they struck deep into my bosom like sharp arrows.

These were not mere words; they were revelations about the creation of the universe that opened the door to a new world. When Jesus spoke, it seemed like a soft breeze, but I took his words to heart and prayed with earnestness strong enough to uproot a tree. Gradually I came into a new realization about God's purpose in creating the universe and His principles of creation.

During the summer of that year, I went on a pilgrimage by myself. I had no money. I would go to homes and ask to be fed. If I was lucky, I caught a ride on a truck. This was how I visited every corner of the country. Everywhere I went, I saw that my homeland was a crucible of tears. There was no end to the sorrowful sighs of suffering from hungry people. Their woeful lamentations turned to tears that flowed like a river."

—Rev. Sun Myung Moon

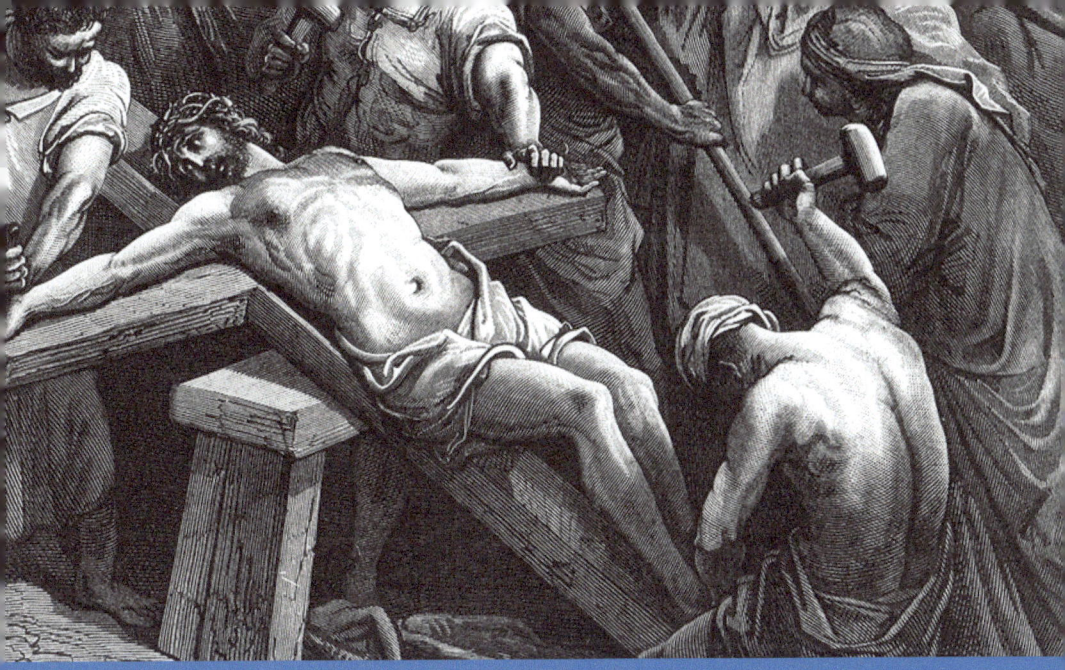

Unraveling the Mysteries of Scripture

From 1935-1941, six years of vigorous prayer, fasting and study, he unravels God's relationship with humankind and develops the fundamentals of the Wolli Wonbon (the Divine Principle).

He studies the Bible and other religious teachings in order to unravel the mysteries of life and human history. He comes to understand God's own suffering and His longing to be reunited with His children. He learns the difficult steps that humankind would have to take in order to return to God and establish true peace.

He intensifies his quest for the truth, spending days and nights in passionate prayer, rigorous fasting and study.

His method is to posit specific questions, research answers in the physical and spirit worlds, and then seek confirmation of those answers through prayer.

On several occasions he is guided directly by Abraham, Moses, Jesus, Muhammad, Buddha and other saints and sages of all faiths, who meet him in spirit and contribute to his understanding of God and the complex history of God's relationship with humankind.

Four years later, at age of 25, he develops the fundamentals of the *Wolli Wonbon*, the original text of the Divine Principle. This will become the core teaching of the Unification faith.

Learning the Amazing Truth

In the beginning of his search for the truth, Sun Myung Moon met Jesus and God spiritually and received their teachings.

"It was when I was sixteen years old that I started experiencing God in a poor situation... From then on for nine years I was always with almighty God and Jesus. Many times I entered into the spirit world. Heavenly Father gradually taught me the amazing truth. It was as if the sun was rising in the morning after a long, dark night. I was able to see the dawn of new, glorious civilization within that truth."

—Rev. Sun Myung Moon

The Divine Principle is Written

1952

The Wolli Wonbon, the original text of the Divine Principle, is handwritten by Sun Myung Moon in Busan, Korea.

(Rev. and Mrs. Moon reviewing the original manuscripts of the Wolli Wonbon.)

After the liberation of Korea in 1945, Rev. Moon begins his public ministry, though the Wolli Wonbon in its completed state is not yet written. Rev. Moon preaches and sermonizes without an official text. After the Divine Principle is finally written, on July 20, 1953, he sends Gang Hyeon-sil to Daegu as the first missionary. This is the first time the Divine Principle is taught publicly.

Also In This Decade

1930   The first World Cup of football is held in Uruguay
1930   March 12: Gandhi's salt march
1931   The Empire State Building opens in New York
1934   Mao Zedong leads the "Long March" of the communist "Red Army" in China
1938   Volkswagen introduces the "Beetle"
1939   September 1: WWII

1940

HAK JA HAN, THE MINISTRY AND PRISON

Japan, Communism and Imprisonment

1941

Sun Myung Moon's involvement in the underground Korean independence movement in Japan and the first of six imprisonments.

After high school graduation, Sun Myung Moon goes to Japan to study electrical engineering at an industrial college affiliated with Waseda University. He keeps three Bibles in his room—one in Korean, one in English and one in Japanese—, which he studies continuously. He is also one of many Christian leaders in the Korean independence movement against the Japanese occupation of Korea.

Young Christians and communists make up the independence movement's strongest leaders. In Japan, some of his closest school friends are communists, and while their atheism pains him, he recognizes their sincere dedication to a Utopian ideal and even defends his communists friends to his Christian friends, saying that they are good people and that Koreans should work together to save their country.

He is eventually arrested and jailed by the Japanese for his student underground activities and tortured for not revealing the names of his collaborators. This is the first of six imprisonments under four governments: Japan, North Korea, South Korea and the United States.

Hak Ja Han is Born

Soon-ae Hong speaks about her daughter's birth.

"My daughter was born in the village named Sinli of Anju district in what is now called North Korea at 4:30 a.m. on January 6, 1943 [by the lunar calendar] when I was 30 years old.

Her father was a disciple of Rev. Young-do Lee when he received a revelation saying, 'Marry a daughter of a man named Yoo-il Hong. Her baby, if it is a boy, will be the king of the universe. If it is a girl, she will be the queen of the universe.' I met him at the end of February and became pregnant at the end of March.

My family believed that the Second Advent would come in a physical body and there needed to be three generations of only daughters who would prepare the foundation for his arrival.

My mother, Won Mo Jo, was an only daughter. I was an only daughter, and my daughter was an only daughter as well.

In my family lineage there were seven generations that performed meritorious deeds. Three generations of the seven had only one daughter respectively.

—Soon-ae Hong

Heaven's Bride Revealed

Hak Ja Han Moon speaks about the search for the heavenly bride.

"I would like to talk about the background of my birth. There were many special dispensational events that took place, secretly, internally, in order to welcome the True Parents here on earth. In Korea there were many special spiritual groups that were completely different from the conventional Christian ones, which just implicitly believed in the Bible and Jesus Christ, hoping to go to Heaven. The spiritual groups existed solely to receive revelations from God, to prepare the way for the coming of the Second Advent here on earth, and to search for and find the heavenly bride."

—Dr. Hak Ja Han Moon

The 38th Parallel

August 15, 1945

Despite the end of the war Sun Myung Moon's fears are realized

"Korea erupts in ecstatic response to the liberation from years of Japanese occupation, but the country is divided in two at the 38th parallel.

The war was coming to an end, and the Japanese police who had imprisoned me were desperate. They tortured me in ways I cannot describe. As soon as I was released in February of 1945, I took all my diaries to the bank of the Han River. There I burned them so they would not cause any further trouble to my friends.

Finally on August 15, 1945, Korea was liberated from Japan. This was the day every Korean had been waiting for. It was a day of tremendous emotion. Shouts of "Mansei!" and people waving the Taegukgi [Korean national] flag covered the entire peninsula.

I could not join in the festivities, however. My heart was deadly serious because I could foresee the terrible calamity that was about to befall. I immersed myself in prayer. Soon after, however, my fears were realized. Although liberated from Japanese rule, our homeland was cut in two at the 38th parallel."

—Rev. Sun Myung Moon

Rev. Moon Teaches the Divine Principle

By 1945 he has systematized his teachings into a text called Divine Principle and he begins his public ministry. The Divine Principle is the fundamental teaching of Reverend Moon and the Unification Church.

Rev. Moon works hard to introduce his new insights to existing Korean Christian churches, but they are not well received. American Christian missionaries in Korea disregard him as an unschooled "country preacher." Korean ministers, jealous of the young man's impact on members of their congregations accuse him of espousing false teachings. Rev. Moon soon realizes that he is headed down the lonely path of a pioneer religious visionary.

Back to the North

Following God's call, Rev. Moon goes back to North Korea to preach and is imprisoned, tortured and left for dead.

In 1946 he receives God's call to go to communist North Korea to preach. Since before World War II, the center of Korean Christian activity has been Pyongyang, now the capital of North Korea; it is called the "Jerusalem of the East." Among the spirit-filled churches are many with strong messianic expectations. Some of these churches have received revelations that the Messiah will be born in Korea, and they are directed in various ways to prepare to receive him.

He begins to teach publicly, despite the dangers presented by the communist-dominated government. As a controversial preacher, Rev. Moon is an easy target. He is one of the first religious figures to be imprisoned by the communists. He is tortured and believed to be dead, his body tossed into the prison yard. Some of his followers find him and carry him away to tend to his broken body. Miraculously, Reverend Moon survives and regains his strength. Undaunted, he begins preaching in public once again.

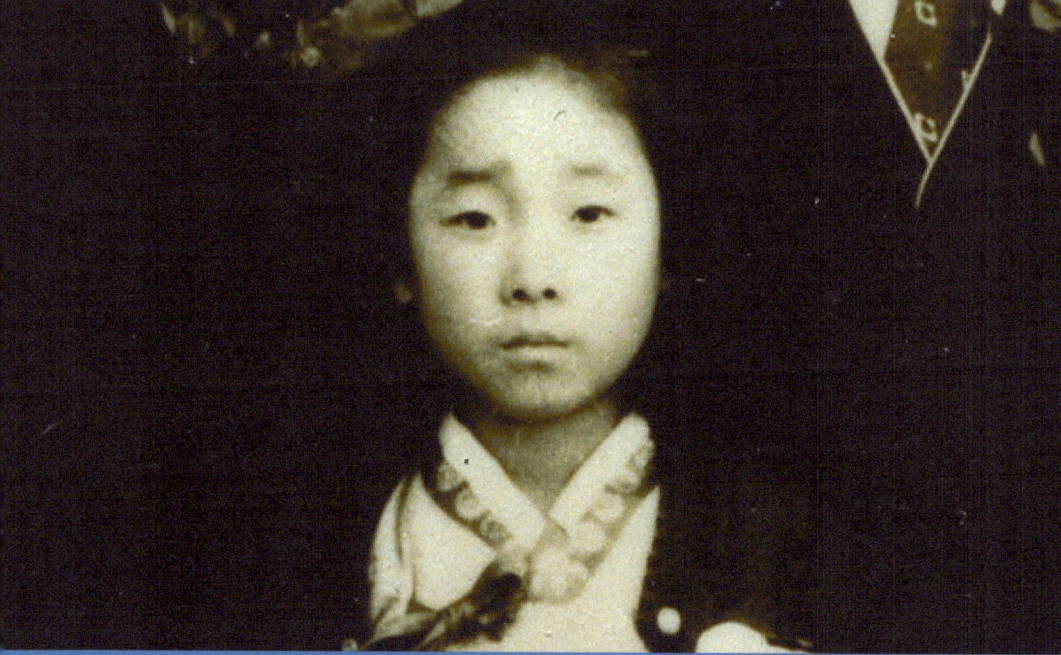

Hak Ja Han Escapes North Korea

Hak Ja Han Moon's mother speaks about escaping North Korea

"When my daughter was six years old, she and I were arrested by the communist regime in North Korea. We were kept in prison for 11 days. In those days I knew through revelation that the Lord of the Second Advent was in the South. I keenly felt that I would have to go to find this person.

My physical father told his wife and me to escape to the South. My daughter was a very pretty girl with a fine physique. Her manner of speaking was also very good. She spoke very carefully. The communist government officials were kind to her and sold her apples and other goods, although they were not kind enough to sell anything to us grown-ups.

My physical mother, my six-year-old daughter (who was to marry Rev. Moon) and I escaped from the residential area at midnight and walked to the border between North and South Korea. When we were crossing the border, my little girl asked me, "Do we still have to sing those songs praising Kim Il Sung? Can I sing the songs of South Korea?" When I said to her, "Yes, you can," she started singing. While we were walking in the border area, the soldiers of the South started shooting. But when they heard Mother singing, they stopped. We told them that we had come from the North. They welcomed us warmly, saying, "You must have had many difficulties in coming with such a small child." They gave us the money necessary for us to travel to Seoul, the capital of South Korea."

—Soon-ae Hong

Finding Disciples in Prison

April 1948

Rev. Moon is wrongly imprisoned and is moved from one prison to another until he arrives in Heungnam Prison where he stays until he is freed by UN forces.

Rev. Moon is arrested a second time and sentenced to five years hard labor at a prison camp in the northeastern port city of Heungnam where prisoners are deliberately worked to death. Few last more than six months. Rev. Moon, however, survives for nearly three years. Many of his fellow prisoners look to him for spiritual strength and become his disciples.

A Single Grain of Rice

1948

Throughout his ministry, Rev. Moon speaks a great deal on solving world hunger. There are many instances in his life when he goes hungry and witnesses many of his people die from hunger.

"Our meal rations in Heungnam Prison consisted of less rice than it took to fill two small bowls. There were no side dishes, but we were given a soup that was radish greens in saltwater. The soup was so salty, it made our throats burn, but the rice was so hard we couldn't eat it without washing it down with the soup.

No one ever left even a single drop of the soup. When we received our bowl of rice, prisoners would put all the rice into their mouth at once. Having eaten their own rice, they would look around, stretching their necks sometimes to watch how the others ate. Sometimes someone would put his spoon in someone else's soup bowl, and there would be a fight. People were so desperate that if a prisoner died at mealtime, the others would dig out any rice still in his mouth and eat it themselves.

The pain of hunger can only be known by those who have experienced it. When a person is hungry, a mere grain of rice becomes very precious. Even now, it makes me tense just to think of Heungnam. It's hard to believe that a single grain of rice can give such stimulation to the body, but when you are hungry you have such a longing for food that it makes you cry. When a person has a full stomach, the world seems big, but to a hungry person a grain of rice is bigger than the earth."

—Rev. Sun Myung Moon

Also In This Decade

1940   The first freeway is built in Los Angeles
1941   First casino opens on what would become the Las Vegas Strip
1945   January 1: WWII ends
1947   November 29: Creation of Israel
1948   Mahatma Gandhi is assassinated by a Hindu extremist
1949   NATO is formed by western European countries and USA
1949   China invades Tibet

1950

THE KOREAN WAR AND
THE UNIFICATION CHURCH

Helped by My Uncle

1950

"At the time of the Korean War, many Koreans suffered a lot, but thanks to my uncle, I had relatively less trouble fleeing from the war. My uncle, Sun-jeong Hong, had graduated from university in Japan and was working as a medical officer in Seoul.

We stayed in Daegu [a city in the southeast part of South Korea], and my grandmother and mother opened a small store. I was less than ten years old at the time, and I had been playing in front of the store when a passing ascetic or perhaps a Buddhist priest asked my mother if I was her daughter.

She answered yes, and he told her not to exchange me for ten sons and to raise me well because I was precious. He also told her that I was destined to marry at the age of seventeen, even though I was then less than ten years old and it was a time of war and everyone was suffering. He added that my husband would be much older than I. I don't know if he said this because it was wartime, but in any case he also said that my husband would be a man of considerable means who would dominate the land, sea and air."

—Dr. Hak Ja Han Moon

The Korean War Begins

June 25, 1950

A global conflict erupts on the Korean peninsula.

The North Korean army invades the South in a lightning attempt to unify the entire peninsula by force. United Nations and U.S. forces, under Gen. Douglas MacArthur, rescue the beleaguered South.

One month after the capture of Seoul, UN and ROK forces reach the gates of Heungnam prison. The camp is liberated just hours before Rev. Moon's scheduled execution. *(The photo shows the Heungnam docks being bombed by the US naval forces.)*

Rev. Moon does not flee to the South with the other prisoners. Instead, he returns to Pyongyang and spends forty days searching for his scattered congregation. He eventually finds a few of his members and then travels south on foot with two of them. One of them has a broken leg and protests that he will slow the party down. Rev. Moon insists on bringing him and for the long trek alternately pushes him on a bicycle and carries him on his back.

The House on the Hill

1951

Won Pil Kim and I broke rocks, dug the earth, and carried up gravel. We mixed mud and straw to make bricks, then stacked them up to make the walls. We got some empty ration boxes from an American base, flattened them out, and used them as the roof. We laid down a sheet of black plastic for the floor.

Even simple huts are built better than this. Ours was built against a boulder, so a big piece of rock stuck up in the middle of the room. Each morning, when Won Pil Kim went to work at the American base, I accompanied him to the bottom of the hill. When he came home in the evening, I went out to greet him and welcome him. The remainder of my time I spent writing the *Wolli Wonbon*.

When we built the mud-walled house and began the church in Beom-net-gol, there were only three people to hear me preach. For me, however, I was not talking to just those three people. I thought to myself, "Though they cannot be seen, I am preaching to thousands, even tens of thousands." I envisioned as I preached that all humanity was in attendance. These three people sat before me while I conveyed the words of the Principle in a loud, booming voice.

The World Converges in Korea

July 27, 1953

On July 27, 1953, representatives of the United States, China and North Korea sign an armistice agreement, ending the fighting between North and South Korea. Reverend Moon is now 33 years old.

"Sixteen countries, led by the United States, sent armed forces to the aid of South Korea.

The division of the Korean Peninsula was created by the history of struggle between good and evil. When the Korean War broke out, the Soviet Union, China and other communist countries came to the aid of North Korea. In a similar way, sixteen countries, led by the United States, sent armed forces to the aid of South Korea.

Also, five countries sent medical teams and twenty nations provided war supplies. What other war in history involved so many countries in the fighting? The reason that the entire world became involved in a war that took place in the tiny country of Korea is that this was a proxy war between the forces of communism and the forces of freedom. It could be said that Korea came to represent the world and that good and evil fought fiercely on its soil.

—Rev. Sun Myung Moon

Preparing for the Future

1953

Hak Ja Han Moon's mother speaks about nurturing her daughter's spiritual life.

"In 1953 I took her to Jeju Island, where we lived a very simple life—a life of prayer. The older she grew, the more beautiful she became. She did so well at school and was so popular that she was the target of a lot of attention. I knew that boys would try to tempt her by writing letters and other things, so I let her quit school when she was a sixth-grader. I took her to Jeju Island, where we lived a very simple life—a life of prayer.

As I had received revelations that the heavenly kingdom on earth would be realized in Korea and that the Messiah would come to Korea, I raised my daughter in such a way that she could not be attracted to anybody else until she could meet the Messiah. In other words, I took a child to an isolated island and gave her spiritual training. I trained her severely, even when she cried."

—Soon-ae Hong

The Unification Church

May 1, 1954

The Holy Spirit Association for the Unification of World Christianity is founded in Seoul.

On May 1, 1954, in Seoul, Rev. Moon founds the Holy Spirit Association for the Unification of World Christianity—the faith community that is popularly called the "Unification Church."

The church immediately attracts followers from Ewha University, a major Christian women's school closely linked with the government and Protestant denominations. Because many students are joining, the school sends professors to investigate. When several professors also join, instead of sincerely welcoming this new church, the school persecutes it.

At the same time, alarming news stories abound. Rev. Moon is thrown in jail, to be released weeks later when no charges can be verified. His release, however, receives scant notice in the press.

Amid this severe persecution, Rev. Moon nurtures a growing community of faithful disciples, known as the "weeping church." By 1957, churches are established in thirty Korean cities and towns.

Why We Call Ourselves the "Unification" Church

"In May of 1954, we rented a house in Seoul and hung out a sign that read "Holy Spirit Association for the Unification of World Christianity." We chose this name to signify that we belonged to no denomination and we certainly had no plans to create a new one.

"World Christianity" refers to all of Christianity worldwide and both past and present. "Unification" reveals our purpose of oneness, and "Holy Spirit" is used to denote harmony between the spiritual and physical worlds built on the love of the father-son relationship at the center. Our name is meant to say, 'The spiritual world, centering on God, is with us.'

In particular, unification represents my purpose to bring about God's ideal world. Unification is not union. Union is when two things come together. Unification is when two become one."

—Rev. Sun Myung Moon

The First Time We Met

March, 1957

Hak Ja Han Moon recounts her auspicious first meeting with her future husband.

"The first time I met Father, he looked at me and asked, 'What is your name?' I said, 'My name is Hak Ja Han.' Then Father closed his eyes and meditated for a moment and said, almost to himself, but I could still hear, 'Oh, God, you have given such a woman, Hak Ja Han, to me and to this country of Korea.' At that time I couldn't understand how this religious leader should have such a special feeling and revelation concerning my future."

—Dr. Hak Ja Han Moon

My Heart Was Already Resolved

"In those days our church members loved Father, but they were scared of him as well. Yet I had no fear of him. I felt that True Father was exactly like my maternal grandfather and would not get upset with anything I said. I suppose some people around me might have thought, "For such a young lady, she is incredibly bold." Yet at that moment I felt as if True Father were my grandfather, father, groom, brother, and even my son.

Adam and Eve fell when they went against God's Word. Yet I thought of it this way: Even if God had not warned them, they should have had the thought, based on the working of their original minds, to observe God's Word, since they were living at a time when they could directly converse with God. I grew up already thinking about God's providential history. So when I met with True Father I had already made this resolution, "I will end, within my lifetime, the history of restoration through indemnity that God has walked in suffering; I will do this myself" I did not think this way because someone taught me to; I made this resolution on my own. The reason I could do so was because I knew God."

—Hak Ja Han Moon

A Sincere Student

Hak Ja Han attends Hyochang Elementary School in Seoul. After leaving Seoul she continues her schooling, even though she moves several times—to Daegu, to Seoguipo on Jeju Island, and to Chun-cheon in Gangwon Province. Her report card from Bongeui Elementary School in Chuncheon records that she is "very pure, kind and polite, shows a noble attitude, the most feminine among the students in the class." When she graduates from that school, she is given an award as an honor student.

Hak Ja Han then attends Seong-jeong Girls Middle School from April 1956 to March 1959. She then enters Saint Joseph's Nursing School in Seoul, which today is the Catholic University Nursing School.

My Desire to Help Others

"In middle school, I was the head of the Student Activities Council. I remember the time when I had to stand on stage and explain the council's decisions to all the students of the school. I later heard that after my speech, my Korean teacher and other teachers remarked, "Wow! Hak Ja, you were great!" People around me always had the impression that I was a quiet and well-mannered student, someone whom it was difficult to be close to. I guess they were surprised that a person such as me could give a public speech, although it was only a simple presentation. This was my first experience speaking in front of many people.

When I started high school, it was not very long after the Korean War had ended. I remembered how all the streets had been filled with people injured because of the war. Children orphaned by the war, and even children with parents, suffered greatly from hunger and disease. People were unable to get any treatment when they fell sick. I felt so sorry for them. I wanted to heal their pain; that is why I decided to attend nursing school. I wanted to find a way to help them. "

—Dr. Hak Ja Han Moon

My Life of Faith While Studying

"My teachers loved and protected me at every school I attended. Some teachers said, "You are not like most children these days. Go out and get involved." It was not that I had a lot of worries on my mind. I just liked to sit and stay quiet. Even during adolescence, when I was growing into womanhood, I never worried about my life because my grandmother and mother, who were always attending heaven, taught me to live in faith.

I was known as a student who liked reading and music in a comfortable and quiet atmosphere. Also, people had the impression that I was quite intellectual. I was not extremely emotional or excitable. Come to think of it, I might have given a first impression of being a little cold. In the dormitory I lived like a nun. My life was sheltered from the secular environment, like a flower blooming in a greenhouse. Only later did I realize that my life was that way to separate me from the fallen world. It was heaven's preparation, so that one day I could meet the Lord of the Second Advent and become his Bride.

Under my mother's strict education, I spent my time immersed in reading books of various kinds. My friends said, "Although you are very prim and proper, you will actually be the first of us to marry." I have not thought much about my student days since the Holy Wedding, so I cannot remember much about that time."

—Dr. Hak Ja Han Moon

Also In This Decade

1951	The first commercial computer is built, the Univac
1955	The first McDonald's restaurant opens near Chicago
1955	Disneyland opens in Los Angeles
1955	Martin Luther King organizes non-violent protests against racial segregation
1955	November 1: Vietnam War
1959	The Dalai Lama of Tibet flees to India
1959	38 million Chinese starve to death because of the 1959-62 famine caused by Mao's "Great Leap Forward"
1959	War erupts between Soviet-sponsored regime of North Vietnam, led by Ho Chi Minh, and the USA-sponsored regime of South Vietnam

1960
TRUE PARENTS

Holy Wedding

April 11, 1960

In his fortieth year, Rev. Moon held the Holy Wedding Ceremony blessing himself and Hak Ja Han in holy matrimony.

With the Holy Wedding of Rev. Sun Myung Moon and Hak Ja Han, the positions of True Father and True Mother are established. Five days later three couples are blessed. These are the first couples to receive the Marriage Blessing from Rev. and Mrs. Moon, who stand in the position of "True Parents".

On May 1, 1961 an additional 33 couples are blessed in marriage. The Marriage Blessing tradition of the Unification faith is the celebration of receiving a blessing from God, our Heavenly Parent, centering on the ideal of true love. It is the beginning point in the process of becoming true husbands and wives and in establishing God's ideal, the Kingdom of Heaven on earth and in the eternal hereafter, through the building of families centered on God.

The Marriage Blessing ceremony has expanded to become an inter-religious affirmation of the universal importance of marriage and family. Blessing ceremonies are held regularly to this day with hundreds of thousands of couples participating either at the main ceremony in South Korea or via satellite in ceremonies around the world.

Accepting the Role of True Mother

September 8, 1960

"Mother was very young when she was blessed, and she said that she had no experience with men.

With a prayerful mind focused just on doing God's Will, she accepted everything in faith and service to God, and came to be the True Mother of the universe."

—Rev. Sun Myung Moon

I Understood I Was Being Prepared

"I can still vividly recall the moment True Father saw me in my student uniform and closed his eyes in gratitude to God for guiding me to him. I always had the feeling that God prepares everything that He deems necessary, especially when I think of how He shaped my character and guided the way I had been living my life. When Isaac went up the mountain with Abraham to make an offering to God, he asked his father where the offering was. Abraham simply replied that God would provide. Yet, although Isaac was just a young boy, he had already figured out his situation.

Likewise, from my childhood I intuitively sensed that I must fulfill something important in the future. I would say that subconsciously I understood that I was being prepared to become the Bride of the Returning Lord. My path was already decided, and I was born with the destiny to go that way.

When I met True Father, I already knew providential history. I had not studied the Principle, but I knew about the history of the providence of restoration through indemnity. That is why I thought to myself, "In order for True Father to be able to proclaim that he has completed his mission as the Messiah, I must offer him my effort in support. I will not shift that responsibility to any other person. As for myself, I will accomplish that responsibility. I will advance the Will for as long as I live and bring it to pass. Without a doubt I will defeat Satan." It is for this purpose that I have dedicated my mind and body and sacrificed my entire life."

—Hak Ja Han Moon

The First World Tour

February, 1965

Answering a call from God, Rev. Moon undertakes the first world tour, going to Japan, North and South America, to nations in Europe, to Egypt and the Middle East.

"In 1965, I embarked on my first trip around the world. My suitcase was filled with soil and stones from Korea. My plan was that, as I traveled around the world, I would plant Korea's soil and stones in each country to signify Korea's linkage to the world. For ten months, I toured forty countries. My second destination was the United States. I entered the country through the airport in San Francisco, where I was met by our missionaries.

During the time I was touring America, I felt strongly, 'This is the country that manages the whole world.' We rented a station wagon and drove day and night. We didn't waste time sitting down to eat. If we had two slices of bread, a piece of sausage, and some pickles, then that was plenty of food for a meal. We ate, slept, and prayed in that small car.

After the United States and Canada, I went to Central and South America, and then on to Europe, to Egypt and the Middle East and completed my tour after ten months.

When I returned to Seoul, my suitcase was full of soil and stones from 120 locations in forty countries; wherever I planted those small pieces of Korea I collected soil and stones to bring back with me. I connected Korea to these forty countries in this way to prepare for the day in the future when the world of peace would be realized centering on Korea. I began preparations to send missionaries to those forty countries."

—Rev. Sun Myung Moon

The 2000-Year-Old Olive Tree

1965

Visiting Jerusalem on the tour, Rev. Moon makes significant symbolic and ceremonial gestures towards the unity of the Unification of the Abrahamic faiths.

"Judaism, Islam, and Christianity are sharply divided against each other in today's world, but they share a common root.

I first set foot in Jerusalem in 1965. This was before the Six-Day War [of June 1967, in which Israel defeated Egypt, Jordan and Syria], and Jerusalem was still under Jordan's territorial control. I went to the Mount of Olives, where Jesus shed tears of blood in prayer just prior to being taken to the court of Pontius Pilate. I put my hand on a 2,000-year-old olive tree that could have witnessed Jesus' prayer that night. I put three nails in that tree, one for Judaism, one for

Christianity, and one for Islam. I prayed for the day when these three families of faith would become one. World peace cannot come unless Judaism, Christianity and Islam become one. Those three nails are still there.

Judaism, Islam and Christianity are sharply divided against each other in today's world, but they share a common root. The issue that keeps them divided is their understanding of Jesus. To address this problem, on May 18, 2003, I asked that we de-emphasize the cross in relations among the Abrahamic faiths. Thus, we enacted a ceremony of taking down the cross. We brought a cross from America, a predominantly Christian culture, and buried it in the Field of Blood in Israel. This is the field that was bought with the thirty pieces of silver that Judas Iscariot received for the betrayal of Jesus that ended in Jesus' crucifixion."

—Rev. Sun Myung Moon

Developing a Heart for Others

October 20, 1968

Mother has been taking Unificationists from other countries shopping, spending time choosing things for them to wear. Even when she is tired, she goes out for long periods of time with them. I was surprised and impressed, and I thought about how beautiful it was. Eventually, Mother will get old and need a cane, and I can imagine young people joyfully following her around, like kids in a toy shop! What a beautiful scene that will be! That could only happen in the name of love."

—Rev. Sun Myung Moon

Also In This Decade

1961	Amnesty International is founded by British lawyer Peter Benenson to promote human rights worldwide
1962	Brazil declares football player Pele an "official national treasure"
1963	President John Kennedy is assassinated
1963	Bob Dylan releases "Blowin' In The Wind"
1963	Bell Labs introduces the touch-tone phone
1963	"Beatlemania" sweeps the world
1964	The Shinkansen (a bullet train) is inaugurated in Japan
1966	The first "Summer of Love" of the hippies is held in San Francisco
1966	Mao launches the "Cultural Revolution" that will kill one million people and destroy thousands of monuments
1966	There are 2,623 computers in the USA (1,967 work for the Defense Department)
1967	The first "automatic teller machines" is deployed by Barclays Bank
1968	Martin Luther King is assassinated
1969	Gary Starkweather of Xerox invents the laser printer
1969	USA astronaut Neil Armstrong becomes the first man to set foot on the Moon

1970

FIRST WORLD TOUR, AMERICA AND THE MARRIAGE BLESSING

777 Couples' International Marriage Blessing

October 21, 1970

The 777 Couples' Blessing was the first Marriage Blessing Ceremony to include international couples.

Rev. Moon later explained that all nations of the world could be connected through this Blessing:

"The 777 Couples' Blessing made it possible for all the families, tribes and nations of the world to be linked to God. The 777 Couples opened such a door; so when we follow the 777 Couples, we will end up in the Kingdom of Heaven.

"That's why the Unification Church, based on the 777 Couples' Blessing, could begin to work on the worldwide level. A new origin was established in 1970."

Campaigns in America

December 18, 1971

Reverend and Mrs. Moon arrive in the United States with their children and begin their world-level ministry centering on America. Through the early 1970s he undertakes national speaking tours on the themes of "Christianity in Crisis" and "Day of Hope."

Rev. Moon conducts four separate public speaking tours of the United States in 1973-74: a 21-city Day of Hope tour, a 32-city Day of Hope tour, a 10-city "Celebration of Life" tour and a culminating 8-city Day of Hope tour. These tours are much larger than the original seven-city tour of 1972. Following completion of the 21-city and 32-city tours, Rev. Moon has spoken publicly in all fifty states. Well before the Celebration of Life tour and the culminating eight-city tour, the Unification Church attains national exposure.

Missionaries in Communist Europe

October, 1973

Pioneers who sacrificed everything for the sake of the world

"Unificationists who went as missionaries to communist countries could not even tell their parents where they were going. It was as if they were entering the lions' den. The number of missionaries going to communist countries, however, kept growing.

Then in 1973, there was a terrible incident in Czechoslovakia where thirty Unificationists were taken into custody. One Unificationist, Marie Zivna, lost her life while in prison at the young age of twenty-four. She was the first martyr who died while conducting missionary work in a communist country. In the following year, another person lost his life in prison. Each time I heard that one Unificationist had died in jail, my entire body froze. I could not speak or eat. I couldn't even pray. I just sat motionless for a while, unable to do anything. It was as if my body had turned to stone. I fell into a sorrow that seemed to have no end, as if I had been thrown into deep water.

I saw Marie Zivna before me in the form of a yellow butterfly. The yellow butterfly that had escaped Czechoslovakia's prison fluttered its wings as if to tell me to be strong and to stand up. By carrying on her missionary activities at the risk of her life, Marie truly had been transformed from being a caterpillar to being a beautiful butterfly."

—Rev. Sun Myung Moon

Forgive, Love and Unite

November 30, 1973

At the height of the Watergate scandal, the Unification Church places ads in major newspapers urging Americans to fast, pray and "forgive, love, unite."

In November 1973, during the critical time period of the Watergate scandal, the Unification Church issues a statement entitled "Forgive, Love and Unite," calling upon Americans to unite together around the Christian spirit. This statement in support of President Richard Nixon is aimed at the American conscience, asking, "Is there anyone, among reporters of The Washington Post and leaders of the anti-Nixon movement, who could throw the first stone because they were without sin?"

Rev. Moon explained: "We keep on criticizing and the nation sinks; we criticize some more and the nation falls even further, deep into greater peril. Now is the time for America to renew the faith expressed in her motto, 'In God We Trust.' This is the founding spirit that makes America great and unique. America must unite in her Christian tradition of love and forgiveness in the face of the grave crisis created by the Watergate scandal. America must live for the Will of God, 'Forgive, Love and Unite!'"

This show of support for President Nixon brings public and media attention in the United States to Rev. Moon and the Unification Church. After President Nixon's resignation, a widespread attack is launched in earnest against the Unification Church.

President Nixon Thanks Rev. Moon

February 1, 1974

During the Watergate scandal, Unificationists around the United States and in other nations take up Reverend Moon's call for Americans to "forgive, love and unite" around the U.S. president. This culminates in hundreds of Unificationists gathering on the steps of the U.S. Capitol from July 22 to 24, 1974, with each participant fasting for three days and praying for one U.S. senator or member of Congress.

On February 1, 1974, President Richard M. Nixon invites Reverend Moon to a meeting in the White House and thanks him for his support. During this meeting President Nixon remarks, "All my work had one purpose: to re-establish the morality of America and restore it to be a country in line with God's Will."

The American Movement Expands

April 30, 1974

The Unification Church establishes the Unification Theological Seminary. In succeeding years, the church acquires four additional substantial properties in New York.

Rev. Moon has been searching locations up and down the Hudson River suitable for educational purposes. The former St. Joseph's Normal Institute in Barrytown site has mountains, water and woods all visible, and he explains this is one of the criteria for successful education. Rev. Moon visits the site seventeen times before deciding on the purchase. The "Founder's Rock" marks the place where that decision was made.

It includes 250 wooded acres bordering the Hudson River 90 miles north of New York City and the historic Massena House, a Hudson River mansion originally constructed in 1796, where 10-year-old Theodore Roosevelt spent the summer in 1868.

Unification Theological Seminary (UTS), which now offers fully accredited bachelors, master's and doctoral degree programs, opens its doors on September 20, 1975, and has graduated some 1,500 students. In recent years the Barrytown facility hosts matching convocations, Marriage Blessing education workshops, and sports festivals.

In the following two years, the Unification Church acquires the New Yorker Hotel, the Manhattan Center, the Tiffany Building and the former Columbia Club headquarters on 43rd Street.

Hope Culminates at Madison Square Garden

September 18, 1974

Rev. Moon delivers a speech at Madison Square Garden on September 18, 1974, in New York City, culminating his "Day of Hope" speaking tours which had begun nearly two years earlier.

Representative Unificationists from each of the forty nations where the Unification Church maintained missions in 1974 and remaining American Unificationists — in all, about 2,000 — converge on New York City for a final week-long blitz prior to September 18. Unificationists "wallpaper" Manhattan with 80,000 two-by-three-foot posters with a portrait of Rev. Moon advertising "September 18 Could Be Your Re-Birthday." The New York Times reports, "His face is everywhere, it seems."

The turnout at Madison Square Garden is astounding. At a kick-off banquet held in the Waldorf Astoria hotel the previous evening approximately 1,600 prominent New Yorkers have a chance to see and hear Rev. and Mrs. Moon. The following night, Madison Square Garden is filled to capacity, with an estimated 10,000 to 35,000 ticket-holders turned away. True Father speaks on "The New Future of Christianity." He proclaims Jesus did not come to die on the cross," that the crucifixion was the "secondary," not the "original" mission of Christ, that the Lord would return "as the Son of Man in the flesh," and that "that day is at hand." With nearly two hundred journalists in attendance, widespread publicity helps ensure success in other cities. The pattern of overflow crowds and continued publicity is repeated throughout the tour.

1,800 Couples Blessed in Marriage

February 8, 1975

Rev. Moon explains the significance of the 1,800 Couples' Marriage Blessing to Unificationists.

"You must realize that you are the most blessed couples in the world. Now that the Unificationists have made their debut, first on an individual and then on a family basis, not only the members of my family but all members of the church should make themselves known throughout the world.

Since this is God's will, we must become living monuments that represent and testify to this victory on the family level; thus, we can finally expand our families on earth centering on True Parents."

—Rev. Sun Myung Moon

The International Relief Friendship Foundation

August 31, 1975

Founded under the principle of "living for the sake of others," The International Relief Friendship Foundation, Inc. (IRFF) is organized in 1975.

IRFF is created to provide humanitarian relief to people around the world who have been devastated by poverty, illness, natural disasters and conflicts.

Approaching the end of the millennium, IRFF expands its vision and works toward sustainable development and personal empowerment through people helping people.

Organizing adolescents and young adults in particular, IRFF develops numerous service learning projects through which volunteers give of themselves to help others while developing their own character through a concerted learning component.

World Peace, My Husband, and the Great Raging Ocean

"The ocean is wide enough to embrace the sky, and seems to become one with the sky when reflecting its light. It is the lowest place that receives water from all over the world.

The ocean embraces everything and begets all life. The ocean appears to be calm and tranquil, but massive, black currents flow and rush thousands of meters deep below the surface. When the raging waves and tsunamis rise, everything becomes swallowed up at once. People cannot see the whirlpools that swirl deep within the sea. This is the way my life has unfolded. Within the providence that rages around me like a typhoon, there have been many unspeakable stories unknown to anyone but me. I have struggled against that whirlpool and brought victory without being swept away. This is how I was able to achieve so much for world peace together with my husband."

—Dr. Hak Ja Han Moon

America Is God's Hope: The Yankee Stadium Rally

June 1, 1976

Rev. Moon gives a public speech at Yankee Stadium in New York appealing to America to turn back to God. Yankee Stadium is the first of two major rallies held in 1976 as part of the Unification Movement's Bicentennial God Bless America Festival.

At Yankee Stadium, Rev. Moon compares himself to a "doctor" or "firefighter" who came from the outside to help America meet its third great "test" as a nation, that of "God-denying" communism.

A rainstorm with strong winds hit the stadium prior to the start of the rally, blowing away many of the decorations. Unificationists rise in their seats or dance on top of the Yankee Stadium dugouts, singing "You Are My Sunshine" until the storm subsides. Approximately 45,000 people attend.

At the time, Rev. Moon's message is translated as "God's Hope for America," but since the original text of the speech in Korean was located, the title Rev Moon himself chose is revealed as "America Is God's Hope!"

Victory in the Nation's Capital

September 18, 1976

The Unification Church holds a rally at the Washington Monument with 300,000 in attendance. Rev. Moon explains that the Washington Monument Rally is the largest religious rally to ever be held in the nation's capital.

In a talk delivered in London two years later, Rev. Moon says:

"The Washington Monument Rally was the final accounting of God's dispensation. The individual, family, tribe, nation and world — everything at one time was offered to God and restitution could be made for all of history. That was the meaning of the Washington Monument rally. It was the final showdown between the satanic world and heavenly world, and because the Unification Church represented the heavenly world Satan mobilized all his power to crush it at the Washington Monument.

I felt that if the Washington Monument rally had been a failure, then the Unification Church would have been crushed. The rally was the culminating showdown of my entire life; no matter how much I had accomplished up until that time, if I had failed then, everything would have crumbled. You can imagine my seriousness. In my opinion, the Washington Monument Rally was a miracle."

Later, Rev. Moon adds:

"I will never forget what happened on that day, September 18, 1976. People started coming to the Washington Monument from early in the morning. Some three hundred thousand people gathered. It was impossible to tell where all these people had come from. They had all different colors of hair and skin. All the races that God sent to earth gathered on that day. It was a rally on a global scale."

Creating the News World Newspaper in New York

December 31, 1976

The creation of a media network is not originally part of Rev. Moon's plans in America, however he recognizes the "awesome power" of the media "to create or to destroy," and launches The News World newspaper as a conservative voice in New York.

In October 1976, Rev. Moon assembles a dozen or so Unificationists with journalism degrees and "sets the deadline" for producing the first issue of a new daily newspaper in New York City by December 31, the last day of the United States' bicentennial year.

The vision of ushering in the United States' third century "with a new era of modern journalism" is compelling. Nevertheless, according to one account, "It seemed impossible to start a daily newspaper literally from scratch, using inexperienced people, in dilapidated offices, in less than three months. Still, on December 31, the presses roll early in the morning and the first issue of The News World hits the streets of New York.

It is the only paper to publish during the New York City power blackout of 1977 and during a later three-month newspaper strike, when its circulation soars to 400,000 daily. The paper's boldest move is to predict a "[Ronald] Reagan Landslide" in a banner headline on Election Day, November 4, 1980, followed by an equally large banner headline the following day which read, "Thank God! We Were Right!"

The News World gives birth to several other New York papers, including Noticias Del Mundo, a Korean-language daily, a Harlem weekly, and a press service, Free Press International. It later changes its name to New York City Tribune and eventually gives way to the media network's flagship newspaper, The Washington Times.

US Government Hearings

November 1977

Rev. Moon is accused of being a South Korean government agent in hearings held by Rep. Donald M. Fraser, Minnesota Democrat, who chaired a subcommittee which ultimately issued a report entitled Investigation of Korean-American Relations; Report of the Subcommittee on International Organizations of the Committee on International Relations, U.S. House of Representatives.

Despite its legal gains, two congressional investigations perpetuated a climate of suspicion and hostility in relation to True Father and the Unification Church. The first was a U.S. House Subcommittee on International Organizations investigation into Korean-American Relations chaired by Rep. Donald Fraser (D-Minnesota.). The committee was determined to establish links between the Korean Central Intelligence Agency and the church.

The other congressional investigation consisted of two unofficial meetings convened by Senator Robert Dole (R-Kansas). The first, a February 18, 1976 "Day of Affirmation and Protest," was previously discussed. It afforded anti-church activists the opportunity to present their grievances to representatives of seven U.S. government agencies. The second was a one-afternoon information session for members of Congress on "The Cult Phenomenon in America" on February 5, 1979. On January 6, 1976, prior to the Day of Affirmation and Protest, Senator Dole wrote a letter to the U.S. Internal Revenue Service (IRS) commissioner stating that an audit of the Unification Church was needed. This set in motion the IRS investigation that eventually led to the indictment of True Father and an 18 month sentence in Danbury Prison.

Also In This Decade

1970 Japan has become the third economic power in the world after the USA and the Soviet Union, having overtaken all European economies

1971 East Pakistan, defended by India, separates from West Pakistan and becomes the independent country of Bangladesh

1971 Film director George Lucas founds the film production company Lucasfilm

1971 Alan Shugart invents the floppy disk

1972 The first video-cassette recorder (VCR) is introduced by Phillips

1972 Nolan Bushnell invents the first video game, "Pong", an evolution of Magnavox's Odyssey, and founds Atari

1972 The Global Positioning System (GPS is invented by the USA military, using a constellation of 24 satellites for navigation and positioning purposes)

1973 The World Trade Center is inaugurated in New York, the world's tallest skyscraper

1974 Richard Nixon is forced to resign after the Watergate scandal

1974 Xerox's PARC unveils the "Alto", the first workstation with a "mouse"

1975 The Khmer Rouge, led by Pol Pot, install a communist regime in Cambodia that will kill 1.7 million people

1976 Steve Wozniak and Steve Jobs form Apple Computer and build the first microcomputer in Jobs' garage in Cupertino.

1977 George Lucas directs the film "Star Wars "

1978 Toshihiro Nishikado creates the first blockbuster videogame, "Space Invaders"

1979 The Soviet Union invades Afghanistan and the USA organizes an Islamic resistance

1980

WORLD MEDIA, DANBURY PRISON AND HEUNG JIN MOON

Spellbound by Mother

February 7, 1980

"I find myself somehow spellbound by Mother! I want to tag along with her whenever she goes anywhere.

I am big and Mother is just a small person, but there is a universe of experience between us. I love Mother beyond all the things I must do in the future or the present. My love for her transcends everything else. Mother is the one who must initiate the leadership in our relationship, not I. I have many different responsibilities and much more to accomplish than Mother in the outside world. However, the woman has the more important role than the man in their relationship."

—Rev. Sun Myung Moon

The Providence of the Ocean

October 1, 1980

Rev. Moon creates "Ocean Church"—a ministry to build personal character and revive and strengthen the boating and fishing industries. This leads to maritime activities in Korea, South America, and U.S. locations such as Gloucester, MA; Hawaii; Alaska; Norfolk, VA; and in 2012, Lake Mead in Nevada

In late summer of 1980 Rev. Moon sponsors the first World Tuna Tournament in the fishing town of Gloucester, Massachusetts, to stimulate interest among Americans, particularly young people, in the ocean.

Then, on October 1, 1980, he establishes Ocean Church. He chooses 24 Unification Theological Seminary (UTS) graduates and 60 Unificationists in supporting roles to pioneer 24 port cities on the East, West and Gulf coasts. He directs them to build a foundation of sixty Unificationists, at which point they are to order ten 28-foot "Good Go" fiberglass boats from the Unification Church-owned fleet and one large stern trawler. He advises the Ocean Church pioneers to "visit the Coast Guard chief, police chief and mayor," telling them that "your sole concern is to revive the fishing industry in America." Rev. Moon tells them that their boats "will be your churches." Unificationists, he says, "will have a regular spiritual life" and "catch more fish than anyone else in the area, even more than people who have been fishing for many years."

International Conference on the Unity of the Sciences

November 7, 1981

Mrs. Moon addresses ICUS about family and God.

"They say that behind every great man is a great woman. In this sense I respect you all very much. You have helped your husbands create many things to help humankind. I also try to be a wonderful helper for my husband. But it is hard because, as you know, his ideals and goals are very high. Sometimes I wonder how good a job I am doing. I never get a report card. If you have the chance to ask him, please do so, and let me know the answer!

Today the world situation is becoming dark. Many families are breaking up. My heart is so sad to see this. I think women must give love and practice a sacrificial spirit. When God dwells in every home, then parents and children will have God's love and hope. With families as the cornerstone of society, then our nations and world will become very beautiful and filled with God's love. We truly will be one family under God."

—Dr. Hak Ja Han Moon

The Washington Times

January 1, 1982

A ground-breaking newspaper in the nation's capital

The Washington Times becomes an influential, conservative voice and alternative to the liberal-leaning Washington Post. It is called the "third most-quoted newspaper in America" after only The Washington Post and The New York Times.

At the time of the founding of The Washington Times, Washington, D.C., has only one major newspaper. Massimo Introvigne, in his 2000 book The Unification Church, said that The Washington Post had been "the most anti-Unificationist paper in the United States."

The Washington Times was unusual among American broadsheets in publishing a full-color front page, along with full-color front pages in all its sections and color elements throughout. Although the USA Today newspaper used color in the same way, it took several years for The Washington Post, The New York Times and other newspapers to do the same.

Injustice Is Served

March 12, 1982

Senator Orrin Hatch, a Republican from Utah, speaks on behalf of Rev. Moon and on the injustice of his case.

"Injustice rather than justice has been served. The Moon case sends a strong signal that if one's views are unpopular enough, this country will find a way not to tolerate, but to convict.

We accused a newcomer to our shores of criminal and intentional wrongdoing for conduct commonly engaged in by a large percentage of our own religious leaders, namely, the holding of church funds in bank accounts in their own names. Catholic priests do it. Baptist ministers do it, and so did Sun Myung Moon.

No matter how we view it, it remains a fact that we charged a non-English-speaking alien with criminal tax evasion on the first tax returns he filed in this country. It appears that we didn't give him a fair chance to understand our laws. We didn't seek a civil penalty as an initial means of redress. Rather, we took a novel theory of tax liability of less than $10,000 and turned it into a guilty verdict and eighteen months in a federal prison.

I do feel strongly, after my subcommittee has carefully and objectively reviewed this case from both sides, that injustice rather than justice has been served. The Moon case sends a strong signal that if one's views are unpopular enough, this country will find a way not to tolerate, but to convict. I don't believe that you or I or anyone else, no matter how innocent, could realistically prevail against the combined forces of our Justice Department and judicial branch in a case such as Reverend Moon's."

—Sen Orrin Hatch

Federal Indictment

May 18, 1982

Religious figures from various faiths join in support of religious liberties and minority rights in the "We Shall Overcome" Rally in protest against the unjust conviction against Rev. Moon.

Indicted on 13 counts of tax fraud, including not paying $7,300 taxes on $160,000 of church funds kept in a bank account under his name, Rev. Moon is found guilty of tax fraud by a jury.

On July 16, Judge Gerard Goettel sentences him to 18 months in prison and issues a fine of $25,000. Despite the outcry from religious groups over the legal implications of the verdict, the Supreme Court declines to hear an appeal.

A letter About Forgiveness to Judge Goettel

June 28, 1982

Mrs. Moon writes a letter to Judge Gerard Goettel, the judge who presided over Rev. Moon's court case.

The letter reads: "Throughout our life together, my husband has always encouraged me with his faith and his compassion.

As you may know, many people have said hostile things to and about my husband. I have never once heard him say one hostile thing back to anyone, or even say one hostile thing about anyone. Many times, when I believed that my husband was being unjustly persecuted, I expected that he would express some negative response. Instead I would find that every time he would give the members of the Unification Church a sermon, it was about love and forgiveness. The message that Jesus Christ taught about loving your enemy has always been a central theme, which he has emphasized."

Blessing in Madison Square Garden

July 1, 1982

2075 couples (a large percentage of the American Unification Church at that time) participates in a record-setting wedding at New York's Madison Square Garden on July 1, 1982. This number eclipses the previous record of 1800 couples married by Rev. Moon in 1975, which is recorded in the Guinness Book of World Records as the largest wedding in history.

Rev. Moon explained to the couples:

"The establishment of happy, righteous families as the source of life, love and joy has been the goal of God and man throughout history. To realize that ideal, each of you has dedicated months and years of preparation, often under very difficult circumstances. We can all be justly proud to meet here together on this day, to add another great building block to the kingdom of heaven on earth.

Until today, the eyes of the world have been upon our church; after today, the eyes of the world will be upon you and your families. Remember that your marriage is not merely "until death do us part," but for all time eternal. Each spouse is a key to ever expanding and deepening our understanding of the infinite God. In your marriage, God's love is consummated and together you are able to receive His total love.

God bless you in all that you undertake, and may He give you the vision and strength you need to realize His kingdom on earth. That is the task facing us all."

The World Media Conference

October 7, 1982
At the 1982 WMC, Mrs. Moon speaks about strength of Korean women.

The 1982 WMC makes this year's topic "Problems of Society and the Responsibility of the Media." Two Hundred and Thirty journalists and scholars from 73 countries attend. During her address, Mrs. Moon speaks about the strength of Korean women.

"Women in Korea are known for three traditional virtues: filial piety toward parents, total fidelity to the husband, and sacrificial love toward the children. Korean women are generally shy and somewhat reticent in their manner, yet many times in the past, when the country's fate was in peril, Korean women stood up bravely, defending their homeland with their lives. There are countless Korean 'Joan of Arc's.'

Just between you and me, I can tell you that the real power in Korea is very much in the hands of women. I would say that Korean wives know how to handle their husbands. All except me, that is. I certainly cannot keep up with my husband, Rev. Moon!"

The Passing of Heung Jin Moon

January 2, 1984

"My wife is a woman of incredible strength, but the death of our second son, Heung Jin, was difficult for us.

It happened in December 1983. She was with me in Kwangju, Korea, participating in a Victory over Communism rally. We received an international phone call that Heung Jin had been in a traffic accident and had been transported to a hospital. We boarded a flight the next day and went directly to New York, but Heung Jin was lying unconscious on the hospital bed.

A truck traveling over the speed limit as it came down a hill tried to brake and swerved into the opposite lane, where Heung Jin was driving. Two of his best friends were in the car with him at the time. Heung Jin cut the wheel to the right so the driver's side took most of the impact from the truck. By doing so, he saved the lives of his two friends. I went to the place near our home where the accident had occurred, and the black tire marks veering off to the right were still visible.

Heung Jin finally went to the heavenly world in the early morning of January 2. He had turned seventeen just a month before. Although you know that life in the spirit world is even more vivid than life here on earth, words cannot describe my wife's sorrow when she had to send a child she had raised with love to the heavenly world before her."

—Rev. Sun Myung Moon

Ballet and the Cultural Arts

May 12, 1984
The Universal Ballet Company is founded.

Rev. and Mrs. Moon are vitally interested in the performing arts. The Universal Ballet Company is officially founded in 1984, and continues to tour the world to critical acclaim.

One of only four professional ballet companies in South Korea, it performs a repertory that includes many full-length classical story ballets, together with shorter contemporary works and original full-length Korean ballets created especially for the company. Julia H. Moon, who was the company's prima ballerina until 2001, now serves as general director.

Rev. Moon Arrives at Danbury Prison

July 22, 1984

Rev. Moon arrives at Danbury Prison on July 20, 1984 to serve an 18-month sentence on wrongful charges of tax evasion. Mrs. Moon shares her message with Unificationists after his arrival at Danbury Prison.

"Let us repent and really renew ourselves so that in this time, not just by word but by deed, we can fulfill God's Will. Before I share a message from Father, I have my own message for you. That is, let us have a moment of true repentance. Let us repent and really renew ourselves so that in this time, not just by word but by deed, we can fulfill God's Will. That is my wish and message to you.

I wish that that day, July 20, 1984, had never existed. I wish that we could eradicate that day totally from the calendar. Until the last moment of his departure from East Garden, Father kept speaking to you and encouraging you. He tried to give you courage and a message of incredible cheer.

Of course, an American prison is different from the kind of prison that Father suffered in previously, such as the ones in communist North Korea and South Korea under a very harsh government dictatorship. It's different from those prisons, yet it is still a prison.

On that day, July 20, I accompanied Father, leaving East Garden at 10 p.m. We arrived at the camp, the place of incarceration—Danbury. I escorted Father all the way until the last minute, when Father disappeared inside the door.

Although I wanted to be strong and determined not to cry, still on the way there, my tears overflowed beyond control."

—Dr. Hak Ja Han Moon

The United Nations—A Landmark Speech

November 6, 1984
Mrs. Moon addresses the United Nations

"My husband is today in the United States federal prison in Danbury, Connecticut. He is in prison because he loves God rather than his own freedom. He is in prison because he loves humanity rather than his own comfort. He is in prison because he is a man of principle rather than a man of popularity. And he is in prison because he lives for history rather than for the present moment. When we look at history, we see that men and women of God and men and women of principle often have walked the path of suffering. My husband is following that tradition."

—Dr. Hak Ja Han Moon

A World Media Association

February 1985

Rev. Moon continues in the pursuit of establishing global media centered on truthful responsible reporting.

From 1982 to 1989, the U.S.-based World Media Association brings hundreds of American and foreign journalists on fact-finding trips to Russia and many of the Soviet republics. Soviet authorities send two representatives to the 1988 World Media Conference in Washington, D.C., twelve the following year, and an agreement is reached to hold the 1990 World Media Conference in Moscow.

In 1987, Rev. Moon founds the Summit Council for World Peace, made up of former heads of state and leaders who have made recognized contributions to peace. They are instrumental in making Rev. Moon's meeting with Soviet leader Mikhail Gorbachev in 1990 possible.

Gazing At Eternity

May 1988

"When I look at Mother and the children, I am gazing at eternity.

She is my God-given wife for eternity, and they are my God-given children for eternity. There are always physical limitations and personality clashes in human behavior, and if you quibble and complain, you can find dozens and hundreds of instances every day. But when you look at eternity and your role of serving others, you bind yourself to these people, and you see only their beauty, grace, and God-given blessing."

—Rev. Sun Myung Moon

Also In This Decade

1980	Ted Turner launches CNN, the first cable TV devoted to world news
1980	Seagate Technology introduces the first hard-disk drive for personal computers
1980	The population of China is one billion
1981	The first cases of AIDS are documented
1981	The compact disc (CD) is introduced
1981	The IBM PC is launched, running an operating system developed by Bill Gates' Microsoft
1983	Apple introduces the "Lisa", the first personal computer with a graphical user interface
1984	Alec Jeffreys in Britain invents the DNA fingerprint that can identify an individual
1984	Indian prime minister Indira Gandhi is assassinated by Sikh bodyguards and is succeeded by her son Rajiv
1984	Canon demonstrates the first electronic camera
1984	Apple introduces the Macintosh, which revolutionizes desktop publishing
1985	The Nintendo Entertainment System is introduced
1985	Microsoft ships the "Windows" operating system
1988	"Morris", the first digital worm, infects most of the Internet
1988	Osama bin Laden in Afghanistan creates Al Qaeda, a worldwide alliance of Islamic fighters
1988	Fuji introduces the first digital camera, the DS-1P
1989	The Berlin wall falls and most communist governments of Eastern Europe fall, thus ending the Cold War
1989	The Berlin wall falls and most communist governments of Eastern Europe fall, thus ending the Cold War
1989	The Soviet Union withdraws from Afghanistan and Afghanistan plunges into chaos
1989	Students protest in Tiananmen Square in China

1990

KIM IL SUNG, MARCH ON MOSCOW AND WOMEN'S FEDERATION

The "March" on Moscow

April 11, 1990

Rev. Moon speaks in Moscow at the World Media Conference and meets with Soviet President Mikhail Gorbachev.

Rev. Moon's remarks are not recorded, however, the next night, following a performance of Korea's Little Angels attended by the First Lady, Raisa Gorbachev, he refers in a concluding speech to the "remarkable meeting" he had with President Gorbachev. While stating that he respects and admires the President's courage and leadership, he also recounts that he "told President Gorbachev that the secret for the success of the Soviet Union is to place God at the very center of every endeavor." He goes on to say that "As a religious leader, I firmly believe that a God-centered world view offers the solution to all problems" while "atheistic theories centered only on man bring disaster and self-destruction in the end."

The Way to Unification of North and South Korea

August 12, 1991

"North and South Korea are divided by a cease-fire line, but this is not the problem.

Once we remove that cease-fire line, we will find an even larger barrier between us and Russia and China. For Koreans to enjoy true peace, we will need to overcome those cease-fire lines as well. It may be difficult, but it is not impossible. The important thing is our attitude.

Today when people ask me what must be done to bring about unification, I tell them what I have always said on this matter: "If South Koreans love North Korea more than they love the South, and North Koreans love South Korea more than they love the North, we could unify the peninsula today."

—Rev. Sun Myung Moon

Return to North Korea

November 20 1991

Rev. and Mrs. Moon travel to North Korea and meet with President Kim Il Sung.

Kim Il Sung directs that Rev. Moon's speech at their official banquet be published in its entirety in North Korea's only newspaper, Rodong Shinmun, and it is, word for word, including all references to "God." He also overrules his own subordinates, insisting that he not only wants to meet Rev. Moon but that he wants "to have lunch with him as well."

Kim Il Sung chooses to meet Rev. Moon at his Hamheung palace, about one hundred and fifty miles from Pyongyang, near Heungnam. In fact, the route from the state guest house to Kim Il Sung's residence passes right by the site of the Heungnam prison and fertilizer plant where Rev. Moon had been imprisoned for two years and eight months from 1948 to 1950.

A Federation of Women

April 10, 1992

Mrs. Moon delivers the WFWP inaugural speech, "Unification of the World and the Responsibility of Humankind," in 113 cities in 12 countries, and in three different languages, within an eight-month period in 1992.

In 1993, she speaks in 43 nations and in all 50 states of the United States. That fall Mrs. Moon addresses a rally of 50,000 women in Tokyo.

"Beloved women of the Unification Church, the Women's Federation is holding today's gathering for Peace in Asia for the important purpose of establishing the Women's Federation for World Peace. In the age of women that is now dawning, Unificationists must embrace our husbands and properly educate our children so that we may be a model movement for practicing true love throughout the world. We must gain the active cooperation of our husbands and children for the development of the Women's Federation for World Peace.

Our women's movement is not for women alone. First, a movement of true love for our husbands and children must bear fruit in ideal families. The ideal families formed in this manner will come together to form ideal nations and an ideal world. For this reason, the Women's Federation for World Peace someday must develop into a federation of families for world peace.

For the sake of world peace, we women must take the lead in government, finance, culture and society. The basic values we should uphold in this federation of women are found in Headwing Philosophy and Godism. These values are what unite left and right and overcome atheist materialism. They are certain to be the guiding ideas of the world of the twenty-first century."

—Dr. Hak Ja Han Moon

The Power of Women Will Save the World

January 7, 1993

"Throughout history, women have been persecuted, but I predict this will change. The coming world will be one of reconciliation and peace based on women's maternal character, love and sociability. The time is coming when the power of women will save the world.

Unfortunately today, many women's organizations apparently believe that standing in opposition to men is the way to demonstrate the power of women. The result is an environment of competition and conflict.

The women's organizations my wife leads, on the other hand, seek to bring about peace on the principle that women should work together, take initiative, and empower one another across traditional lines of race, culture and religion to create healthy families as the cornerstone of the culture of peace.

The organizations she works with do not call for a liberation of women from men and families. Instead, they call for women to develop and maintain families filled with love. My wife's dream is to see all women raised as true daughters with filial hearts who can create peace at home, in our communities, in our nations, and in the world. The women's movement being carried out by my wife serves the goal of true families, which are the root of peace in all areas of life."

—Rev. Sun Myung Moon

The First Korean Woman to Speak at the UN

July 28, 1993

Mrs. Moon speaks about Tribal Messiahship at the United Nations. One hundred and five nations send embassy and consulate representatives, including more than 60 UN ambassadors. His Excellency Stoyan Ganev, president of the UN General Assembly, introduces Mrs. Moon. She is the first Korean woman to speak at the United Nations.

"The time has come for each family to take up the messianic mission of completing the work of salvation all over the world. After restoring your family, the next step is to restore your community, tribe and nation. We call this process "tribal messiahship." In the Completed Testament Age, the mother must unite her children and her husband, and link her family with the True Parents. Already we have sent thousands of tribal messiah missionaries around the world.

In every completed family, grandparents will be in the position of kings and queens representing God and good ancestors. Parents will be in the position of kings and queens representing present humanity, and children will be in the position of princes and princesses representing all future descendants. When all three generations are united, past, present and future will live together in harmony.

With this understanding, it is also my great privilege to announce to you the establishment of the first True Family. My husband and I, together with our children and grandchildren, are absolutely committed to serving God and humankind. These three generations constitute the central root (grandparents), the central trunk (parents), and the central bud (children) of the Tree of Life mentioned in the Bible. It is our sincere hope that you will symbolically graft into this tree by joining us in our efforts to create true families, ideal nations and an ideal world."

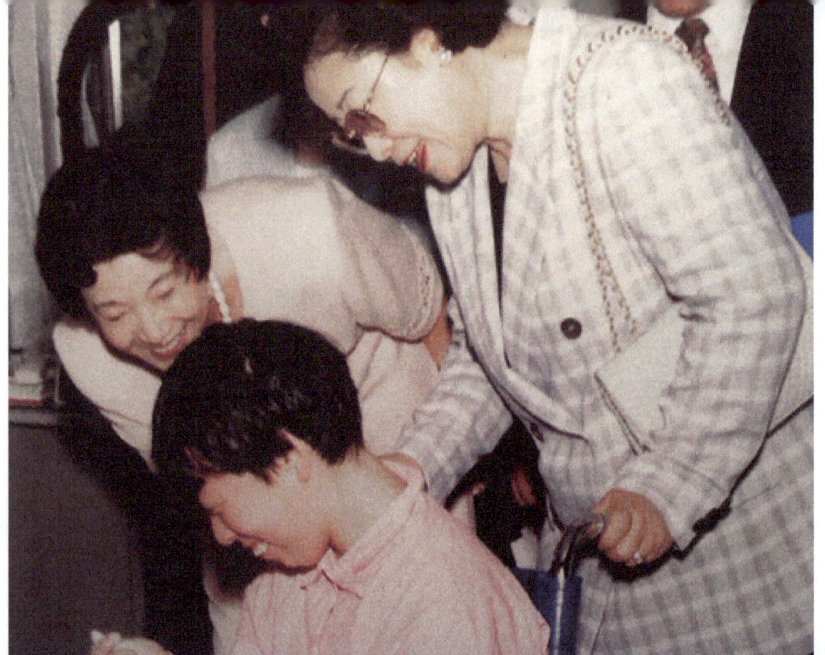

Aewon—True Love in Practice

March 25, 1994

Mrs. Moon establishes the Aewon Volunteer Organization

At the founding of Aewon, Mrs. Moon, states:

"Volunteering your service for the sake of others is the actualization of true love. True love is the sincere gift of a pair of socks to one shivering with cold. True love sometimes means sacrificing yourself for a complete stranger."

Mrs. Moon develops her women's peace initiatives with the heart of a mother, and they receive positive responses throughout the world. She feels that a mother's heart is needed to look after and take care of the impoverished and war-torn countries of the world.

Parents' Day Established As a National Holiday

July 8, 1994

In 1994 Mrs. Moon encourages the establishment of a national holiday to be called "Parents' Day."

In the United States, Parents' Day is held on the fourth Sunday of every July. This holiday is established in 1994 when President Bill Clinton signs a Congressional Resolution into law for "recognizing, uplifting and supporting the role of parents in the rearing of children." The bill is introduced by Republican Senator Trent Lott of Mississippi. It is supported by members of the Unification Church. Parents' Day is celebrated throughout the United States.

The Power of Sisterhood

January 22, 1995

Between January 22 and March 8, 1995, more than 4,000 Japanese women travel to Washington, D.C., and are paired with an equal number of American women in eight separate "sisterhood" ceremonies.

These ceremonies coincide with the commemoration of the 50th anniversary of the end of World War II, and each ceremony builds up to a dramatic "bridge-crossing" during which a representative group of the Japanese delegates meet their American counterparts, bow in respect, and embrace the other.

Following the highly successful Washington, D.C. conferences, the Women's Federation for World Peace (WFWP) sponsors Japanese-American sisterhood ceremonies in eight U.S. cities during the remainder of 1995, with several thousand more women from both countries participating.

In 1996, WFWP conducts a number of "African-American/Caucasian-American" sisterhood ceremonies. Activities in the United States inspire Austrian-Croatian, Czech-German, Russian-German, Hungarian-Slovakian, and Italian-Slovakian sisterhood ceremonies conducted by WFWP chapters throughout Europe.

Family Federation for World Peace and Unification

July 30, 1995

FFWPU is officially launched in Washington D.C.

The Family Federation for World Peace and Unification (FFWPU) is an international organization of families striving to embody the ideal of true love and to establish a world of peace and unity among all peoples, races and religions as envisioned by the Rev. and Mrs. Moon.

The FFWPU is founded in 1995 in order to expand the mission of the Unification Church to create an alliance of people who share the vision of building God-centered families as the basis for healthy communities, stable societies and a peaceful world.

FFWPU champions three ideals mentioned in its title: family, peace and unification. Promoting the values that make for strong families is its central mission. This means encouraging married couples to practice fidelity; it means parents loving and caring for their children, protecting them and educating them to uphold the highest moral standards; and it means children loving and respecting both their parents and grandparents. The FFWPU also seeks a "culture of peace" by supporting inter-religious and international cooperation around the universal themes of family, love and living for the sake of others. The word "unification" in the title refers to the ideal of unity between mind and body, between husband and wife, and between heaven and earth.

Persecuted No More

January 8, 1997

The time is coming when the power of women will save the world.

"Throughout history, women have been persecuted, but I predict this will change. The coming world will be one of reconciliation and peace based on women's maternal character, love and sociability.

The time is coming when the power of women will save the world. Unfortunately today, some women's organizations apparently believe that standing in opposition to men is the way to demonstrate the power of women. The result is an environment of competition and conflict.

The women's organizations my wife leads seek to bring about peace on the principle that women should work together, take initiative and empower one another across traditional lines of race, culture and religion to create healthy families as the cornerstone of the culture of peace.

The organizations she works with do not call for a liberation of women from men and families. Instead, they call for women to develop and maintain families filled with love. My wife's dream is to see all women raised as true daughters with filial hearts who can create peace at home, in our communities, in our nations and in the world. The women's movement being carried out by my wife serves the goal of true families, which are the root of peace in all areas of life."

—Rev. Sun Myung Moon

The Marriage Blessing, True Parents and God

April 1, 1998

Mrs. Moon conducts a speaking tour across America from April 1-16, 1998, speaking on the Marriage Blessing tradition and family life.

"Why do we get married? Very simply, we marry in order to resemble God. God exists as a being of dual characteristics. In God, the dual characteristics are completely harmonized as one. When God's dual characteristics manifest in our world, they do so as man and woman. Accordingly, at the proper time, a man and a woman are like a seed.

Our entire life should be centered on true love. We should be born in true love; we should grow in true love; we should live centered on true love, and we should return to true love when we die. The way of true love is life for the sake of others. This is the purpose of marriage.

The Marriage Blessing and eternal life stem from God working through True Parents' love. Through our union with the True Parents, we can fulfill God's original hope for the individual, the family, the nation, the world and the entire cosmos. Ultimately, we can complete God's ideal of creation. Through True Parents we can find our original homeland, the starting place for the Kingdom of God on earth and in heaven.

With this foundation in place, we can welcome an era in which God is our sovereign. The society that does so will never perish. It will continuously prosper and reach its fullest strength.

I sincerely ask that you contemplate deeply about the meaning of this sermon. If you practice it, you will find the way to receive God's abundant blessing and eternal life."

—Dr. Hak Ja Han Moon

Also In This Decade

1990   The Hubble Space Telescope is launched
1990   February 11: Nelson Mandela released
1991   The World-Wide Web invented by Tim Berners-Lee in Geneve debuts on the Internet
1991   The Soviet Union is dissolved and its states become independent
1994   Nelson Mandela wins the first free elections in South Africa and becomes its first black president
1997   Britain returns its colony of Hong Kong to China, the end of the British Empire
1997   Amazon.com is launched on the web as the "world's largest bookstore", except that it is not a bookstore, it is a website

2000

*ABEL UN, PEACE AND RELIGION,
HYO JIN MOON, AND A GLOBAL CITIZEN*

Ambassadors for Peace

October 20, 2000

Rev. Moon Inaugurates the Ambassadors for Peace program during Assembly 2000, in New York City.

Rev. and Mrs. Moon seek to inspire a broad range of secular leaders with their vision and initiatives for world peace. In August 2000, the Unification Church convenes Assembly 2000 under the theme, "Renewing the United Nations and Building a Culture of Peace." It is attended by dignitaries from over 100 nations, more than 400 "world leaders" in all. The centerpiece of Assembly 2000 is Rev. Moon's keynote address, "Renewing the United Nations to Build Lasting Peace."

In this speech, Rev. Moon proposes the establishment of an inter-religious assembly to serve as a senate or council within the United Nations and that each nation, in addition to its current ambassador, send a religious ambassador or "Ambassador for Peace" to serve as a member of the religious assembly or U.N. senate.

The True Family Ministry

December, 2000
The 5th Annual True Family Values Award Banquet is a precursor to the We Will Stand Tour in 2001.

Chicago is famous for many things: its sports teams, its fierce weather, its gangsters, its politicians and its vibrant and plentiful churches. In the religious community, Chicago also has a phenomenon known as the True Family Values Ministry Awards Banquets, which are celebrations of faith, family and public service. The annual celebration is a tribute to the extraordinary alliance of believers from scores of churches and across racial and cultural lines, denoted by the phrase "True Family Values Ministry." What begins humbly as an educational effort of Unificationist leaders in 1996 leads to historic interfaith and intercultural initiatives that touch hundreds of thousands of lives across the nation and around the world.

"My life was completely changed through my involvement in the True Family Values Ministry," explains Pastor T.L. Barrett Jr., founder and senior pastor of Life Center Church of God in Christ in Chicago. "My involvement with the ministry has not only been a blessing here, it's been a blessing for the nation and the world!"

The foundation of the True Family Values Ministry is the teachings of Rev. and Mrs. Sun Myung Moon, who dedicate their lives to restoring the relationship of individuals and families with God. *(photo from the 2014 Celebration)*

We Will Stand

February 25—April 17, 2001

A declaration to the leaders of American Christianity.

Greatly inspired by the 5th Annual True Family Values Awards in Chicago, Rev. Moon initiates the broadest American speaking tour yet. He has crossed the country many times, but the We Will Stand tour includes a speaking engagement in every one of the 50 American states. The American Clergy Leadership Conference (ACLC) had been initiated in Korea in May, 2000. Now the 120 Christian Ministers who form that group take leadership in co-organizing this huge undertaking.

Choosing to speak as much as possible in churches rather than hotels, Rev. Moon connects substantially with local clergy and guests at every event. ACLC membership rises to 12,000.

The tour is met with a groundswell of support, especially from the nation's African-American churches. Some 21 national evangelists join the tour. In the tour address, Rev. Moon seems more like a father to the audiences, and he reveals God's heart concerning the family, and the importance of healthy marriages. Media coverage of the tour is overwhelmingly postive.

"Who else can come here and say such things to you, black brothers, white sisters, and all different races here?I happen to be yellow-skinned, and I also happen to bring this message from God. That is why I am telling you this so boldly and courageously. I didn't come to America to save only white America. I came to America to save all Christianity."

World Culture and Sports Festival

February 15, 2002

Mrs. Moon speaks about Rev. Moon at the Opening Ceremony of the 2002 World Culture and Sports Festival and of the Inter-religious and International Federation for World Peace.

"I would like to tell you about the Rev. Moon that only I know. After all these years of marriage, I am sure that only God knows him better than I. What do the absolutes that he teaches have to do with his life? I have seen from early morning until late at night his unwavering example of living for the sake of others and seeking to break down all barriers in all spheres of human activity, for the ultimate purpose of breaking down the barriers between humans and God.

When I first met him, the world was still dangerously divided into two armed camps due to the Cold War of the West and East, and this nation of Korea had been tragically torn in two after the Korean War. The first church my husband built was made of discarded cardboard boxes mixed with clay, with a dirt floor. Still, he never doubted God's promise to bring peace and prosperity to this land.

When we first moved to New York and lived in a church facility with several hundred other Unificationists, he was the one who wanted to learn first how to operate the lawnmower, and he was the one who taught himself how to install the carpets. He cut the grass with the heart to make the lawn beautiful in the eyes of God and therefore humans. Every nail in the carpet was the same.

Our life has not been like the lives of others, but as I see the result of his lifelong sacrifice — the millions of families that have begun to follow in this same tradition, and their children and grandchildren — I know that God is truly proud of His dedicated son, my husband, the Reverend Sun Myung Moon.

—Dr. Hak Ja Han Moon

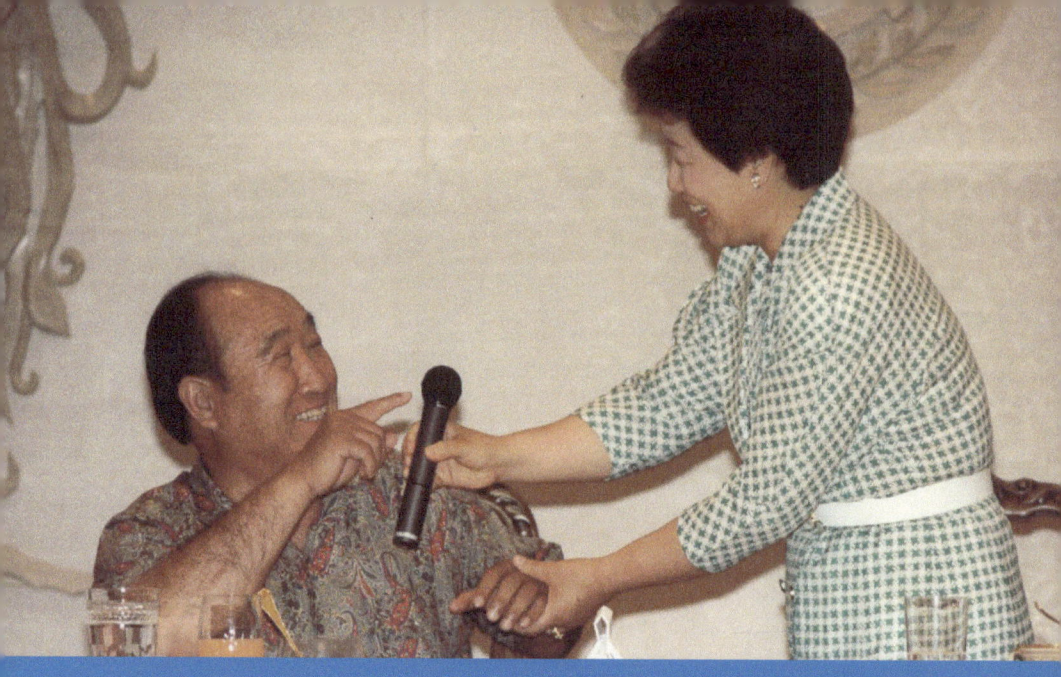

The Way of a Public Life

July 22, 2002

Un Jin Moon shares about her father's lifestyle.

"As human beings, we all have wants and desires. For sisters, it might be jewelry or nice clothes; brothers might wish they had a sporty coup or even just a Volkswagen!

Maybe you would like to have a nice suit, be some kind of leader, or simply be able to support your family. If you have those human desires, then don't you think your parents have desires too? You cannot put Father and Mother in a different category from ourselves; they are human beings, too—they have feelings!

What if Father and Mother got frustrated at all of us do? We get frustrated, and maybe we don't like the food or we just can't seem to get out of bed in the morning, or are just upset; yet Father and Mother have no excuse; they can't be that way. They have no outlet. Even at home in East Garden they have no private life. From 7 a.m. until 12 midnight or 2 a.m. the following morning, Father is up working. They've always led a public life. Even though you might think Father is living in luxurious surroundings, you could take it all away from Father and it would not matter to him one bit.

Actually, Father and Mother have given us all the tools we need in order to save this world; they have shown us the way to live our lives."

—Un Jin Moon

The Sun Moon Peace Cup and Pelé

"Soccer the power to become a force for harmony between countries, races, religions and cultures. I see soccer and peace among countries as potentially powerful partners.

Soccer is a sport in which competition takes place and someone wins or loses, but it also has the potential for significantly influencing countries and increasing their cooperation toward peace. I was told that twice as many people watched the World Cup as watched the Olympics. This provides an idea of how many people around the world love soccer.

Pelé, who was appointed as Brazil's Extraordinary Minister for Sport in 1995, once visited Korea and spent time in the Hannam-dong neighborhood of Seoul. People remember him as the greatest soccer player in the world, but the Pelé I met was a peace activist. He wanted to bring world peace through soccer. When I met him, he laughed as he told me the story of a game in Africa. He said, 'I once played in [the nation of] Gabon in [western] Africa, but the country was at war then. How do you think we were able to play in a place where bombs were exploding all around? Thankfully, there was a cease-fire during the time that we played. That's when I realized deeply that football was more than just a sport in which we kick a ball around. Soccer is a means shared by all people in the world for creating world peace. After that, I decided that I had to carry out a movement for world peace through soccer.' I was so impressed with Pelé in that moment that I firmly grasped his hand."

—Rev. Sun Myung Moon

Women and Peace in the Middle East

May 2004

Mrs. Moon stresses the unique place of women in establishing world peace. The 2004 "Women Building Peace Through Heart-to-Heart Reconciliation and Service" in Jerusalem is especially important.

The Middle East Peace Initiative (MEPI) is launched in 2003 by Rev. Moon as a diplomacy effort to bring a wide range of interfaith perspectives into the center of the search for peace in the Holy Land. Between 2003 and 2008, more than 12,000 members of the clergy, scholars and government officials from around the world participate in MEPI pilgrimages.

The Women's Federation for World Peace initiates a campaign to collect one million signatures for the Women's Middle East Peace Initiative's Declaration for Peace.

The Declaration is carried "around the world in 28 days," taken to Switzerland for the Eighth Women's Conference on Peace in the Middle East, as well as to Israel for the Women of Peace program itself, which is attended by 526 women from 41 nations.

A Federation for Universal Peace

September 12, 2005

Rev. and Mrs. Moon founds the Universal Peace Federation in New York City, and speaks on "God's Ideal Family, the Model for World Peace."

Rev. Moon establishes the Universal Peace Federation on September 12, 2005, prior to the United Nations' 60th anniversary. Its inaugural convocation is held before 376 delegates from 157 nations at Lincoln Center's Alice Tully Hall in New York. Its mission, Rev. Moon declares, is "to renew the existing United Nations and provide a new level of leadership as an 'Abel-type' United Nations."

As part of the launch, he also proposes a "World Peace King Bridge Tunnel" to "build a passage for transport across the Bering Strait." He describes this as "a truly providential and revolutionary project" and envisions it as a crucial "link" in "an international highway system connecting the world as a single community."

UPF is a successor organization to the Inter-religious and International Federation for World Peace (IIFWP, established in 1999). In addition to its UN renewal and Bering Strait initiatives, UPF leads the Middle East Peace Initiative (MEPI), which sponsors interfaith "Pilgrimages for Peace," and its Northeast Asia Peace Initiative (NEAPI), which supports Korean unification.

Speaking Tour in 120 Countries

April 28, 2006

After the UPF kickoff at the Lincoln Center in New York, Rev. and Mrs. Moon immediately begin a worldwide speaking tour of 120 countries.

They travel over 80,000 miles as they visit a different country every day. They are welcomed by presidents, heads of state, leaders of religions, and tens of thousands of ordinary men and women eager to hear their uplifting message of peace and hope.

The next year, Mrs. Moon conducts a U.S. 50-state tour, followed by another U.S. 12-city tour, speaking on the significance of the Pacific Rim in God's providence.

Hyo Jin Moon Ascends to Spirit World

March 17, 2008

Upon his ascension, Rev. and Mrs. Moon offer Hyo Jin Moon this calligraphy:

The lord who will open a gate into the heavenly kingdom, as a son of loyalty and filial piety in the garden that opens the way to the deep, wide and high realms of heaven.

In a deep prayer offered on April 18, 2008, Rev. Moon says:

"Heung Jin has worked very hard as the main responsible person [in the Spiritual World], united with True Parents. From now on, Hyo Jin as the elder brother will cooperate with Heung Jin and even help the people who are living in the most miserable environment.

Hyo Jin is called 'The Lord of loyalty, filial piety and the liberation of the whole spiritual world' in the position of True Parents in the spiritual world. Through the unity of both (Heung Jin Nim and Hyo Jin Nim), the resurrection of spiritual beings will be easier and quicker.

In Hawaii on October 12 of that same year, Rev. Moon adds:

"He lived a most difficult and miserable life in this world but he was splendid. In order for him to liquidate his lack of duty to his parents, he made more than 10,000 songs. In his lyrics, he meant True Father by the words 'My Beloved,' whom he absolutely loved and was united with. He was the elder son whose three generation can be kings.

Hyo Jin knew that he had responsibilities, and he made mistakes. He thought that he could get help from me through True Mother. However, overall, he was a son of filial piety. Mother-son cooperation is a most serious providence at this time. True Children must come to me through True Mother. True Mother's role is to unify them and bring them into oneness with me."

A Helicopter Crash

June 19, 2008

Rev. and Mrs. Moon and others their grandchildren survive a helicopter crash in Korea. They escape with only minor injuries before the helicopter bursts into flames.

Authorities agree that a remarkable set of circumstances coincide, resulting in no fatalities—unprecedented in this type of accident.

The helicopter crashes near the Cheongpyeong Museum. They are returning from a meeting in Seoul, along with ten Unificationists, three of their young grandchildren and three crew members, when they encounter a fog bank as they approach the heliport. When the pilot attempts to take the craft up and out of the pitch darkness, the helicopter tail strikes a tall tree, causing it to plow through the woods at treetop level for a hundred and fifty yards. It finally hits a large tree and crashes in a muddy wooded area near a small stream. An urgent effort to escape the already burning helicopter ensues. Two security staff lift Rev. and Mrs. Moon through the hatch, which fortunately is still accessible. The grandchildren next are lifted up through the same exit. The remaining members of the flight then exit and everyone seeks cover. Twenty minutes after the crash landing, the helicopter explodes. Rev. Moon refers to their survival as "a miracle from God."

The Key to Happiness

January 1, 2009

"Happiness is always waiting for us. The reason we can't get happiness is that our own desires block the way. As long as our eyes are fixed on our desires, they cannot see the path we should follow. We are so busy trying to pick up the scraps of gold lying on the ground near us that we do not see the huge pile of gold that is a little way up the road. We are so busy stuffing things into our pockets that we don't realize that there are holes in those pockets.

I have not forgotten what it was like to live in Heungnam Prison. Even the most terrible place in this world is more comfortable and more materially abundant than Heungnam Prison. Every object belongs to Heaven. We are only its stewards."

—Rev. Sun Myung Moon

Also In This Decade

2000	British and USA biologists decipher the entire human DNA
2000	Boris Yeltsin resigns as president of Russia and is replaced by Vladimir Putin while the Russian economy begins a rapid expansion
2001	Apple launches the iPod
2001	Arab terrorists affiliated with Osama Bin Laden's Al Qaeda organization blow up the World Trade Center, and the USA bombs the Taliban out of power in Afghanistan
2004	Google launches a project to digitize all the books ever printed
2006	North Korea explodes a nuclear bomb
2005	The Internet is used by one billion people
2007	5.4 million people have died in Congo since 1998 due to war, famine and disease
2008	The Large Hadron Collider, the world's most powerful particle accelerator, is inaugurated at CERN
2008	Korean auto-maker Hyundai becomes the fourth-largest automaker in the world behind Toyota, General Motors and Volkswagen
2008	Barack Obama, a black man, is elected president of the USA
2009	For the first time in history, most of the world's population lives in towns and cities
2009	The Internet is used by more than two billion people

2010

**DR. HAK JA HAN MOON,
CONTINUING THE DREAM**

A Peace-Loving Global Citizen

March 9, 2009

As a Peace-Loving Global Citizen is published in Korea and celebrates Rev. Moon's 50th wedding anniversary with his wife, Dr. Hak Ja Han Moon.

The idea of publishing Rev. Moon's autobiography, As a Peace-Loving Global Citizen, is first proposed by Gimm-Young Publishing Company, a leading Korean publisher. Its president, Ms. Pak Eun-ju, a practicing Buddhist, approaches the church in 2008 and obtains access to voluminous source material, notably Rev. and Mrs. Moon's Life Course (12 volumes), a work comprising excerpts from Rev. Moon's speeches arranged chronologically in the form of an autobiographical account.

Unification Church representatives work with the publisher's writers to craft the final product, published on March 9, 2009. It quickly makes Korea's non-fiction best-seller list. On June 1, 2009, the church hosts a commemoration of the autobiography's publication at the Seoul Convention and Exhibition (COEX) Center for 3,500 people, including 200 foreign dignitaries. An English translation is ready by May 2010, and there is a parallel launch event. Many U.S. Unificationists purchase 430 copies, at Rev. and Mrs. Moon's request, for distribution to friends and family. More than 144,000 copies are distributed in Las Vegas alone.

Rev. Moon describes the autobiography as an "honest and candid account." He says it expresses about 80 percent of his life. In one speech he says he has "as much faith" in his autobiography as in the Eight Great Textbooks.

Why Did God Call Me?

December 25, 2009

"Even now, at ninety years of age, I wonder every day why God called me. Of all the people in the world, why did He choose me?

It wasn't because I had a particularly good appearance, or outstanding character, or deep conviction. I was just an unremarkable, stubborn and foolish young boy. If God saw something in me, it must have been a sincere heart that sought Him with tears of love. Whatever the time or place, love is most important. God was searching for a person who would live with a heart of love and who, when faced with suffering, could cut off its effects with love. I was a boy in a rural village with nothing to show for myself. Even now, I insist uncompromisingly on sacrificing my life to live for God's love and nothing else."

—Rev. Sun Myung Moon

The World Tour

April 1, 2011

Rev. and Mrs. Moon embark on a speaking tour throughout Asia, Europe and Africa.

The World Tour runs for four weeks, from April 24 to May 21, beginning on Easter Sunday with a speech to twelve thousand people in Incheon, Korea. Rev. and Mrs. Moon along with members of their family visit and speak in Spain, Italy, Norway, Greece, Turkey, the United Kingdom, Switzerland and Germany. The concluding event is held in Las Vegas on May 21 with some three thousand people in attendance.

According to the hotel staff in Rome, seats are continually add as more than a thousand people come to hear Rev. Moon's speech. A European Leadership Conference is held in conjunction with their visit to Norway and at the Little Angels performance in Berlin, Rev. and Mrs. Moon present medals honoring three people for their peace work.

In London, Mrs. Moon speaks to a large audience in an office in the nine-hundred-year-old Palace of Westminster, which also houses the British Parliament. Seated nearest her are her family members and senior European Unificationists. Labor Party Member of Parliament David Anderson greets Mrs. Moon. In Istanbul, Turkey, Rev. Moon speaks to an audience that includes people from throughout the Middle East

On April 18, 2011, Rev. Moon proclaims the beginning of the Age after the Coming of Heaven on the occasion of the 52nd celebration of True Parents' Holy Wedding ceremony. It is an age in which a new heaven and a new earth are to be established through the recovering of True Love. Thus, this tour is to unfold the lifestyle of the Age after the Coming of Heaven.

What the Ocean Taught Me

July 11, 2011

"The longer a person spends on the ocean, the greater the spiritual aspect of his life will become.

The ocean can be calm one minute but then quickly change its face and send us strong waves. Waves several times the height of a person will rise up above the boat, as if to devour it. A strong wind will tear at the sail and make a fearful sound.

Think of this, though. Even when the waves have risen and a fearful wind is blowing, the fish in the water have no trouble sleeping. They give themselves over to the waves and don't resist them. This is what I learned from the fish. I decided not to be afraid, no matter how strong the waves were. I let the waves carry me. I made myself one with the boat, and we rose with the waves.

Once I started doing that, my heart was never shaken, no matter what kind of waves I came up against. The ocean has been such a wonderful teacher for me."

—Rev. Sun Myung Moon

The Won Mo Design

September, 2011

Rev. and Mrs. Moon unveil the personally designed "Won Mo" boat in Las Vegas.

In September 2011, Rev. and Mrs. Moon unveil a new dimension in the Las Vegas providence with the dedication and launch of the 28 foot Won Mo sports fishing boat. Utilizing an innovative resin mold designed by Rev. Moon as well as helium air tanks making the boats unsinkable, the vision is for Las Vegas to become a hub of family-friendly entertainment that will include world-class shows, fishing on Lake Mead and visits to the majestic natural wonders nearby.

The Won Mo boat is displayed before local officials in a 135,000 sq. ft. warehouse which becomes the International Peace Education Center with educational and residence facilities. This is consistent with Rev. Moon's dual emphases on education and leisure culture/economic activity.

The "Abel" Women United Nations

July 16, 2012

"I would like to emphasize again that the priority of the Abel Women UN should be creating a true family movement that emphasizes living for the sake of others based on true love, and carried out in conjunction with education in proper values.

Women are not here merely to help or to be protected by men; rather, they are independent individuals who as representatives of the feminine aspect of God's nature are meant to make men more complete and manly. Centering on true love, women are men's precious love partners. Men and women are absolutely equal in terms of value.

In the twenty-first century, women should play a major role in world history by serving, together with men, as one of the wheels of the engine pulling forward the construction of a peaceful world. Going beyond a century of power and technology, women will be the central axis in building a century characterized by its loving, peaceful culture, and their role will be more important than ever before.

I sincerely ask you to see True Mother's path as a model for your own lives. She follows the path of a true wife, the path of true daughter, and the path of a true woman leader who will build a unified world where freedom, peace, and happiness in its truest sense, overflow."

—Rev. Sun Myung Moon

The Ascension of a Beloved Husband, Father and True Son of God

September 3, 2012

Rev. Sun Myung Moon dies of pneumonia-related complications at the Unification Church complex at Cheongpyeong, South Korea. Mrs. Moon addresses Unificationists at his Seonghwa Ceremony.

"Today we come to an exceedingly important turning point in God's governance of His providence. It is unprecedented, historic and revolutionary.

My husband, the Rev. Dr. Sun Myung Moon, the returning Lord, Messiah, Savior and True Parent who came as the root of the lineage of original goodness, has departed for the spirit world. Consequently, we now stand at a providential starting point from which we must inherit True Parents' realm of victory and build the ideal kingdom of peace, one family under God.

True Father's Seonghwa brings me, after being together with him my whole life, unfathomable pain and sorrow. It is the same for all of you. Moreover, we cannot begin to fathom the sorrowful heart of God, who is the original substance of eternal love and the True Parent of humankind.

From another aspect, this is also a time of hope. True Father worked in accordance with the heavenly laws — which God established at the time of the creation of heaven and earth — to conclude, complete and perfect all the providential tasks on earth that no one in human history had been able to fulfill. He is now transitioning to the spirit world to exercise dominion over both the spirit and physical worlds and initiate a new dimension of God's providence. No spoken or written language known to human beings can possibly express the flood of emotions we experience as we stand at this juncture in the providence."

—Dr Hak Ja Han Moon

Our Life in the Spiritual World

"The first motto of all the schools I have founded is "Live a life that casts no shadows, as if you were under the sun at high noon." A life without shadows is a life with a clear conscience.

When we finish our life here on earth and go to the spirit world, our entire life will unfold before us, as though it were being played back on videotape. Whether we go to Heaven or to Hell is determined by how we live. So we need to live spotlessly clean lives, casting not even the smallest shadow. This is the importance of living a life with a clear conscience."

—Rev. Sun Myung Moon

Mrs. Moon Invests in Education

February 20, 2013

Mrs. Moon speaks at the Scholarship Awards Ceremony of the Wonmo Pyeongae [Eternal Parent's Love] Foundation.

"Dr. Sun Myung Moon devoted his lifetime to building a global family, and his desire is embodied through the Wonmo Pyeongae Foundation. The foundation will focus on the role of educating talented youth, as well as contributing to society through business education. We must educate our younger generation in the tradition of living for the sake of the world and for others. Please become peace-loving global citizens who inherit Dr. Sun Myung Moon's will."

Sunhak Peace Prize

February 2013

In February 2013, Mrs. Moon officially proposes the creation of the prize.

The Sunhak Peace Prize is proposed by Mrs. Moon to recognize key movers and shakers for peace who are leaving a lasting legacy, and to honor selfless individuals who recognize family values as cornerstone of society.

The Sunhak Peace Prize Foundation is established two years after its proposal. It gives an annual award to individuals or organizations that have contributed substantially to peace and human development for the sake of future generations. It continues the legacy of Sun Myung Moon's lifelong dedication to peace and promotes the vision of "one family under God", a world wherein all people live together as one global family, transcending barriers of race, religion, nationality and culture.

Sponsored by the Wonmo Pyeongae Foundation, the Sunhak World Peace Prize is an international award that is given to an individual or organization who has contributed to the realization of peace for humanity in accordance with the ideals of True Parents, and whose actions have brought positive impacts to multiple nations, races, religions, and ideologies.

UPF World Summit: An Assembly for World Peace

February 23, 2013

A total of 600 worldwide leaders, including former and present political and religious leaders, join the UPF World Summit, an assembly for world peace, and symbolically light candles and ring the "bell of peace."

"My husband and I share a clear vision for the Asia Pacific Era and the rise of a new global organization that will bring together all the nations, religions and peoples of the world. While we have always had great respect for the United Nations, and always believed that such an institution was linked to the providence of God, the time is ripe for change. As you know, the United Nations intervened when this nation of Korea was invaded by North Korean communists. Young men and women from 16 nations came to Korea, putting their lives at risk for people they did not know, in order to save this nation. In the process of saving this nation, those UN forces also saved my husband from certain death in a brutal North Korean communist prison camp.

As much as we love and respect the United Nations, we also recognize that the UN needs renewal and reform. Rev. Moon envisioned a new kind of United Nations, which he often called the "Abel United Nations."

—Dr. Hak Ja Han Moon

The Holy Scriptures

June 10, 2013

Mrs. Moon and 1,000 Unificationists attend a joint event to celebrate the 60th anniversary of the Founding of the Holy Spirit Association for the Unification of World Christianity (HSA-UWC) and the publication of new editions of Holy Scriptures.

She explains "The root of Unification Church and of Family Federation for World Peace and Unification (FFWPU) is the church and scripture, and at its center are True Parents.

The 60 years of Father's work is like precious jewelry. I am so happy and truly appreciate that these beautiful jewels are not in disarray but are orderly. It is the time when we need to accelerate our actions in the era of Cheon Il Guk, and these books will serve as the actual center, fruit and pillar of Cheon Il Guk.

The New Holy Scriptures will have three volumes: the Cheon Seong Gyeong (drawn from the entire library of all True Parents' speeches), the Pyeong Hwa Gyeong (a collection of all True Parents' speeches to public audiences) and the Cham Bumo Gyeong (covering True Parents' life and work, in their own words."

In September of the same year, Mrs. Moon commissions a series of three volumes called the Holy Scriptures of teachings compiled from decades of sermons to capture the essence of her husband's unique understanding of the heart of God and to add a few significant insights of her own.

She directs that the work be completed during the traditional three-year period of mourning for Rev. Moon.

The Holy Scriptures is a set of three volumes of True Parents' messages — the Cheon Seong Gyeong, the Pyeong Hwa Gyeong and the Cham Bumo Gyeong— the Cham Bumo Gyeong being the latest volume.

Aloha Workshop

Summer, 2013

Mrs. Moon holds a thirty-day workshop for the third-generation of her family, Rev. and Mrs. Moon's grandchildren, at Hawaii King Garden.

Mrs. Moon presides over the first ever" True Parents' Aloha Reunion" at Hawaii King Garden, where her grandchildren come to learn more about the Divine Principle and True Parents' lives in a familial, embracing, and supportive environment. From 2014 onward, the Aloha Reunion is open to young Unificationists as well, reflecting Mrs. Moon's desire to personally invest in the younger Unificationists and future leaders. In 2014, a select group of young Unificationists travel to Hawaii where they are taught directly by Mrs. Moon.

"My message today for you is to become water that spreads out the true love of our Heavenly Parent and the True Parents of Heaven, Earth and Humankind…. Hence, I would like to entertain great hopes of your big dreams… As you compare the nature here and that of your countries, please reflect on the field you will study and how you can become leaders that can realize the ideal of the Kingdom of Heaven that our Heavenly Parent originally created, that same beauty within your countries. Please be determined to become like pure water."

In 2015, the reunion is renamed the "Aloha Leadership Workshop," and a slightly older demographic of Unificationists (16- to 20-year-olds) attend. In 2016, the Aloha Winter Workshop coincides with Mrs. Moon's visit to the United States to attend the inauguration of IAPP and the dedication of the Hyo Jeong East Garden Museum.

The aim of the workshop is to enable the young people to inherit True Parents' traditions and filial hearts, experience God's heart at the time of the creation by interacting with nature in Hawaii and to guide them in nurturing the dream of becoming Cheon Il Guk leaders.

"She Is Indeed True Mother"

January 1, 2014

Yeon Ah Choi Moon, Mrs. Moon's daughter-in-law and widow of Rev. and Mrs. Moon's eldest son, Hyo Jin Moon, shares her experiences with Mrs. Moon.

"I feel that she acts and thinks like True Father. True Father always lived centered on Heaven, investing all his heart in everything that he did with very little sleep at night. Because of this, those who worked closely with him had difficulties both physically and spiritually when following him.

After his Seonghwa, True Mother said, 'I never slept over three hours because I attended True Father all my life.' Now that he is in the spirit world, we would like her to rest a little. She is 70 years old, so she should spend time resting and taking care of her health."

—Yeon Ah Choi Moon

Holy Marriage Blessings Continue

February 13, 2014

Mrs. Moon continues to officiate the Holy Marriage Blessing Ceremonies.

On February 12, 2014, some 20,000 couples from 194 countries say, "I do" at a Marriage Blessing Ceremony that spans the globe. Mrs. Moon officiates in person for 2,500 couples—including 50 couples from the United States—at the Cheongshim Peace World Center in South Korea while couples throughout the world join via satellite. The ceremony is conducted on the first anniversary of the Cheon Il Guk Foundation Day Commemoration Ceremony.

"What do you think will happen if people from the United States and Russia marry across the boundaries of their nationalities through an international and cross-cultural marriage Blessing? The two nations will become one family under God, who is the eternal, absolute Lord of all creation. How could anyone harbor antagonism toward, much less point weapons at, a nation in which many millions of grandchildren from their own lineage make their home?

Some may laugh and say that it is impossible, but I tell you that the holy task of restoring the 6.5 billion people of the world to the true lineage of God, and fulfilling God's wish for the ideal Kingdom of Heaven that is the sacred reign of peace on earth, is being carried out in all corners of the world."

—Rev. Sun Myung Moon

I Have But One Life Goal

February 24, 2014

"I have but one life goal: to live in utmost gratitude. Today I will be more grateful than yesterday; tomorrow I will be more grateful than today.

However, I must confess to all of you that even though I feel that I have to be strong, determined and constantly moving forward, it is sometimes inevitable that I feel rather weak, sentimental and emotional, and that is the truth of the matter.

I always think: What is the true way to pursue a life of faith in God? If we have a way of knowing the Will of God precisely, then to fulfill that Will is, of course, ideal. But in many cases we do not have that good fortune. So we stumble, wander and go back and forth—we all have some feeble tendencies. For that reason I feel the best virtue in pursuing the path to Heaven is to obey. Obey God, obey His Will.

When it comes to laying a strong tradition in our life of faith, it usually takes the woman, not the man, to really lay the strong tradition. Women have experienced giving birth and raising children. Suppose one of your children is not as smart as the others. That doesn't mean you can mistreat this one. Parental love, particularly mother's love, goes especially to the one who is not as good as the other children. If we try to avoid a difficult struggle rather than face it, this does not benefit us or anyone else. Father's life has always been that way. There have been many opportunities for Father to avoid difficult circumstances and take the easy way, but he has never avoided any troublesome situations. He always faced them in light of the Divine Principle."

—Dr. Hak Ja Han Moon

Founding Cranes Club in Las Vegas

December 19 and 21, 2014

The inaugural Cranes Club Conference is held at South Point Hotel in Las Vegas.

Cranes Club is an organization that provides a supportive network of young Unificationist professionals who aspire to contribute their expertise towards the successful establishment of Cheon Il Guk. Young business people from around the globe attend the inaugural conference.

Mrs. Moon addresses Cranes with the following words:

"What is your dream? God created the cosmos. At the time, He had a big dream. You understand that from the Divine Principle, right? What is God's dream? Through Adam and Eve, God wanted to become a True Parent. That is God's dream. But in the face of that great dream, the first human ancestors failed to fulfill their responsibility. They could not fulfill God's dream.

You are living at the same time when True Parents are alive. You have been breathing the same air, what does that mean? You are like the ancestors. You are the central figures. You can be the beginning of your lineage, and you should not be the kind of person that your family should be ashamed of. No matter where you are in the world, no matter what you do there, you should always know that there are people who could gain new life through you, and that you have such a responsibility.

When I see you so young, I feel energy. And I really want to embrace all seven billion people of the world. Until then, what do you think my position is? The position of True Parents is the position of the king of kings, and if you can expand your environment....you should make a lot of effort for that so you can attend True Parents. You should be so busy. That kind of effort is happy effort."

International Peace Education Center

May 28, 2015

On Thursday, May 28, 2015, the International Peace Education Center (IPEC) has its grand opening and sanctification as a new beacon of hope on the horizon of God's providence.

Unification Church leaders from Korea, Japan and America, Unificationists who donated to IPEC, members of the Generation Peace Academy and Universal Peace Academy, 7-day Divine Principle Workshop participants, several news teams from around the world and Unificationists from throughout the states welcome Mrs. Moon to the sanctification ceremony for IPEC. Upon arrival, the 7-day Divine Principe Workshop participants, some of whom are guests and see Mrs. Moon for the first time, witness a crowd of Unificationists eager to express their love to True Parents.

True Mother gives a tearful prayer, asking our Heavenly Parent for forgiveness for not being able to do more and do it faster. Following the prayer, there is a ribbon-cutting. Mrs. Moon's demeanor is of complete seriousness over the occasion.

The International Peace Education Center continues to hold Divine Principle and other educational programs.

1,000-Day Memorial for Sun Myung Moon

May 30, 2015

Rev. Moon's 1000 day Memorial Celebration is the first official event held at the International Peace Education Center (IPEC). More than 2,000 people attend. So many people are eager to see the newly finished center that four overflow rooms are completely packed.

People have traveled from near and far to welcome Mrs. Moon. She asks everyone to think very seriously about America's responsibility, especially in its responsibility to the unification of Korea.

"When we move to a new house, in order to adapt to the new house, we need a lot of time to adapt to the new surroundings and that's how we feel today; this new home is our home, in our hearts and bodies. Today is the 1000 day memorial. It is a special service of Jeongseong (devotional offering) for True Father's ascension memorial. Of course, when you think about it, you realize how much Heavenly Parent and True Father have yearned and prepared for this very moment.

It is not for America to live for its own sake but to live for the sake of the world, of others, that is why God blessed this nation of America; however, America has had many challenges in fulfilling this responsibility. That is why True Father came to the American continent and really worked to help America to fulfill this heavenly responsibility. For 40 years True Father invested his blood, sweat, and tears in America.

Today is a special day. True Father is here with us, and he is looking at all of you with a very happy heart and he is wishing all of you can fulfill your blessed responsibility and will, without fail, be centered on Heavenly Parent and together realize one world centering on Heavenly Parent. We are going to do our very best!"

—Dr. Hak Ja Han Moon

Global Top Gun in Korea

August, 2015

The first Global Top Gun (GTG) workshop in Korea gathers 190 youth and leaders from Europe, Korea, America and Japan. The workshop includes Divine Principle lectures and a pilgrimage of Holy Sites.

On August 9, 2015, participants of the global Top Gun workshop embark on a pilgrimage to nine Holy Grounds throughout Korea. In the span of five days, they visit nine key places that played a significant role in the history of True Parents' lives and mission.

"You are the first graduates of GTG. There are many Top Gun graduates in Korea and Japan, but can I expect more from you? I always told you that you are different. It has been 6000 years of biblical history. Human history will have been much longer than that. God had a dream. God created heaven, earth, and all of humankind with this big dream in mind. God planned to work together with humankind to achieve this dream.

"In this generation, everything will be short lived if you go alone. You must go together. This is the same for all the nations of the world. Even great countries that have a large population like America, China, or India cannot go alone. You must communicate with those in other countries around you. You must unite. Do you understand? There True Parents are at the center. Thus, there is a cure, internally and externally, that can solve all the problems in every part of the world. I hope that you will stand in the center of the mainstream of Cheon Il Guk and shout out before the world. I hope you will become proud first Global Top Gun graduates."

—Dr. Hak Ja Han Moon

Peace Road

June - August 2015

Rev. Moon's 1,000 Day Memorial Ceremony is marked by numerous momentous events in Las Vegas, including the Peace Road 2015 World Launching Ceremony held at the newly opened International Peace Education Center and attended by Mrs. Moon and members of her family.

The Peace Road 2015 World Launching Ceremony is a global project with the vision of unifying Korea and creating world peace. It began in 2013 to honor True Father's legacy and inherit and develop his ideas of peace. Its foundation lies mainly in the World Peace Highway project, which True Parents officially suggested in 1981 in Seoul, Korea, and at the Universal Peace Federation (UPF) Foundation Assembly in New York in 2005.

About 500 persons gather at the 2015 World Launching Ceremony, including FFWPU regional presidents, special emissaries and national leaders.

Peace Road is inspired by the International Highway Project (IHP), a visionary call for a super highway free of tariffs and passports, linking the entire globe. Rev. Moon first proposed it at the International Conference on the Unity of Sciences in 1981.

Mother Moon moves the project forward in 2015 by suggesting we take small steps throughout the world. Thus is born Peace Road. Cyclists tour their cities, states and regions to publicize the International Peace Highway in over 30 nations, from South Africa to Chile, Germany to Korea, and in 25 cities across America. On August 28, 2015, the epic Peace Road journey reaches its finale in Seoul.

Yankee Stadium Anniversary at Belvedere

June 5, 2016

3,000 Unificationists gather at the Belvedere Estate in Tarrytown, New York to celebrate the 40th Anniversary of True Parents' landmark rally at Yankee Stadium on June 1, 1976.

Though more than three inches of continuous rain, thunder and lightning was in the forecast, the rain holds off right until the very last moment when Mrs. Moon leaves the stage after her speech—and then the heavens open and the water comes down in sheets.

In her address, Mrs. Moon says:

"America is a chosen and blessed nation of God, and as we all know, with great blessings come great responsibility. America is to be the elder son nation, working with God and keenly aware of his burning desire to build his kingdom right here in America.

Yet, somehow, America is in danger of losing its ways. Most of the problems of 1976-youth immorality and family breakdown, secular humanism and individualism, and the declining influence of true religion-are all problems today as they were then. America needs to realize that it must unite with True Parents, sent by God to be the returning Messiah and the parents who can bring the divided human family back together again!"

In addition to this celebration, on September 17, 2016, over 4,000 people gather at the National Mall in Washington, D.C. to celebrate the 40th anniversary of True Parents' groundbreaking Washington Monument Rally in 1976. Among those in attendance are many of the veterans of the original rally, standing together with their children and grandchildren.

International Association of Parliamentarians for Peace

November 30, 2016

Mrs. Moon inaugurates the International Association of Parliamentarians for Peace (IAPP) in the Kenny Caucus Room in Washington D. C.

A bipartisan group of former U.S. Congressmen Dan Burton (R-IN), Bill Delahunt (D-MA), Todd Tiahrt (R-KS) and John Doolittle (R-CA) invites colleagues from Capitol Hill to a reception in the Russell Senate Office Building held in honor of 56 legislators from 56 countries who came to Washington D.C. to form a global organization of parliamentarians who want to work beyond the boundaries of partisanship to address pivotal issues involving terrorism, the environment, freedom of conscience and other pivotal issues common to all nations.

"Dr. Moon is truly an amazing woman, and one that I deeply respect," Senator Orrin Hatch of Utah says. "She is a champion of peace and someone who I hope will have a lasting impact for years to come."

Mrs. Moon speaks of the responsibility of global leaders to work together to create peace and calls for a new and international commitment to unselfish good governance.

"We look at this world and see unspeakable, inarticulate misery happening all around the globe. This is impossible to solve with mere human power. All of you esteemed leaders, members of parliament, beloved leaders who have gathered here, members of parliament from all over the world, your responsibility is great and important. You are extremely important, especially in this era, when a new providence is unfolding. More than just one person, you who represent the people, you are the mediator. God needs each one of you."

A New Generation at East Garden

December 4, 2016

Three hundred youth from all over the country and abroad, aged 13-40, gather at East Garden with the purpose of connecting in heart with True Parents and to give Mrs. Moon hope for America. The event is hosted by CARP and Cranes Club.

Mrs. Moon shares a message which gently educates participants on the history of the providence and God's work to find the Only Begotten Daughter, drawing parallels from history on the importance of not being ignorant of the role we play and heeding us to truly understand the time we live in.

"Wherever you may be—whether you are studying, whether you are developing your talents and abilities—you always should think this way: 'I am doing this such and such, and I would like to offer this to True Parents. What do True Parents wish of me?'

You have such a beautiful future ahead of you. You have the potential to greatly contribute to the providence as outstanding leaders and outstanding, talented people." She reminded us that we are young, with so much life ahead of us, and that "all of you are truly blessed by the backing of heaven; there is nothing you need to be afraid of."

As Mrs. Moon leaves the room she greets one young man, Noriaki To of New Jersey, with a loving touch on the cheek and the room explodes in cheers; what one receives is felt by all.

Dediction of the Hyojeong East Garden Museum

December 6, 2016

Unificationists gather at East Garden to say farewell to True Mother. On her last day in New York, she offers a profound prayer of dedication at the opening of the Hyojeong East Garden Museum. It showcases the early years of the American movement under True parent's leadership.

Our dear, most beloved Heavenly Parent, the Parent of Heaven, Earth and Humankind: Here at the East Garden Holy Ground we offer this place, the old house where we began the providence in America, as a museum. During the arduous course of the Providence of Restoration, You gave fallen humanity hope. However, the first providence for the advent of the Messiah, Savior and True Parent through the people of Israel ended in failure. No one in all the history of humankind knew how great Heaven's effort and suffering had been.

Heavenly Parent, You, however, with an unchanging heart, restarted the providence of salvation through Christianity and prepared for two thousand years for the returning Lord, who Jesus promised would come again. Therefore, You raised America to play the central role in the providence by becoming a nation that could prepare for and receive True Parents, the Second Coming of the Messiah.

Rally at Madison Square Garden

July 15, 2017

In a highly-successful rally in New York, True Mother delivers a challenge to America and the world to stand up for peace. The American membership responds to the call, and in many ways they see the rally as a restart of spirituality in their lives.

True Mother delivers the keynote address in the "Peace Stars with Me" interfaith rally at the illustrious venue of Madison Square Garden on July 15. Co-sponsored by FFWPU, the Universal Peace Federation (UPF), Women's Federation for World Peace (WFWP), and the American Clergy Leadership Conference (ACLC), the program makes a call for peace starting with ourselves and expanding outward into our communities, the nation and the world.

The program included Paula White, who delivered the invocation at President Trump's inauguration, Grammy Award winners Bishop Hezekiah Walker and Yolanda Adams, a 2,000 Voice Choir, 200 Praise Dancers, and 600 youth and young adults from the Hyojeong weekend workshop. True Mother challenges those present to "be lights to the world with redoubled courage."

Hyo Jeong Workshop

July 14-16, 2017

Mrs. Moon meets with youth and young adults on the final day of their workshop.

From July 14 to 16, over 500 youth and young adults from all around the nation and the world enjoy a fulfilling weekend in which they connected with one another, True Parents, and True Parents' family, learning the meaning of hyojeong, a heart of filial piety. The connection between the young Unificationists and True Mother would grow even greater at the Victory Celebration on July 16. On this beautiful Sunday morning at East Garden, they have the blessing of joining in a special gathering with True Mother. With the young Unificationists huddling around True Mother, the physical and spiritual closeness between them at its height, True Mother expressed how proud she was of every one of them.

She thanked them for their participation at the Madison Square Garden Rally and encouraged them to strive for personal excellence, while focusing on a life to service to all people.

Peace Starts With Me

December 4, 2017

At Mrs. Moon's invitation, American Clergy travel to Korea to participate in in the 2017 Interreligious and International Clergy Conference for World Peace.

On behalf of the American Clergy Leadership Conference, we wish to profess our profound gratitude and appreciation for welcoming us. The very name that you have given so many of the buildings, Hyo Jeong, speaks of filial heart; a heart of a son, or daughter for their parents.

There is an expression that goes: If the shoe fits, wear it. Well, True Mother, the shoe fits for you and True Parents as Messiah; the shoe fits you and True Parents as Returning Lord, the shoe fits for you and True Father standing together as the Lord of the Second Advent.

The shoe fits for you to be the Only Begotten Daughter of God. The shoe fits, and so you must wear it. You must wear it because if we get lost, if we get hung up in titles, we will miss the profound love that emanates from the heart of you and True Father, the True Parents of Heaven, Earth, and Humankind.

What I have seen in True Parents is they have become, already, what we hope to be. True Mother, we love you. We love you madly. The same shoe has been worn by Christianity for so long that it has lost its sole/soul; that it is no longer life giving in so many ways. True Parents, True Mother, you have brought us new life, and we will be forever grateful to you. Whenever we remember God, we will call your name. Ommohnim—Cham Ohmohnim, Gamsahamnida.

—Archbishop George Augustus Stallings Jr.,
Co-Chairman, ACLC

Mrs. Moon at the Africa Summit 2018

January 18-19, 2018

At the Africa Summit 2018 in Dakar, Senegal with a thousand African leaders in attendance, Mrs. Moon laments Africa's history of suffering and expresses her hope for Africa to begin a new, heavenly era.

Following her speech, Macky Sall, the President of Senegal, thanks Mrs. Moon and her desire to see the people of Africa live in happiness, peace, and prosperity.

The next day, Mrs. Moon gives a heartfelt prayer for its ancestors and a new, heavenly Africa at the Island of Gorée, the largest slave-trading center on the African coast between the 15th and 19th centuries.

"Christianity did not know Your deep will or Jesus' essence and they left a sorrowful history here in Africa and on Gorée Island. Where did Jesus' words of "Love your neighbor as yourself" go? How could they treat people in this way because of differences in skin color? Please remember the people of Africa who have endured and waited for more than five hundred sorrowful years.

"Beloved Heavenly Parent! Today, in the name of True Parents, I liberate the sorrowful spirits of Gorée Island and through a spiritual workshop conducted by Heavenly Parent, they can be resurrected as good spirits and return to earth and be with their descendants so that Africa can become an Africa that can realize the dream of one human family centered on Heavenly Parent and become the light and lamp of the world. Let us cooperate enthusiastically to achieve a world of no more conflict, suffering, or war—one world of complete harmony and unification centered on Heavenly Parent."

—Dr. Hak Ja Han Moon

America is Ready

March 16, 2018

National leaders and representatives at the 2018 Famicon conference in Las Vegas greet Mrs. Moon during a surprise visit. She expresses her trust in the American movement, which encourages unity with True Parents.

Mrs. Moon is very clear in her message to Famicon participants: "Just as there is only one Heavenly Parent, there is only one True Parents of Heaven, Earth and Humankind." Thus, it is only by uniting with them and Heavenly Parent that the nation, and eventually, the world, can be brought back to God.

"I spoke to all of you that I would build and prepare a foundation that would enable all of humanity throughout the world to experience internally and externally the achievements of True Parents, agree with True Parents and understand easily their providence. Did I achieve this goal or not?

"Furthermore, how would the world of peace that Heavenly Parent and humanity yearn for look like? …I am working so hard [to achieve this world]; should you or should you not expand Heaven's foundation in your respective nations and throughout the world?

"It is because I saw that potential [in America] that I suddenly came here. We shall realize the restoration of the nation and the restoration of the world without fail."

—Dr. Hak Ja Han Moon

Also In This Decade

2010	Winter Olympics—Held in Vancouver, Canada
2010	Haiti Earthquake affects more than 3 million people
2010	British Petroleum oil platform explodes into the Gulf of Mexico. The worst oil spill in history
2010	President Barack Obama withdraws U.S. troops in Iraq—fulfilling his campaign promise
2011	A massive tsunami caused by an 8.9 magnitude earthquake devastates Japan
2012	London Olympic Games
2012	Vladimir Putin is elected as Russian President
2012	Whitney Houston passes away at the age of 48
2012	Obama is reelected for a second term as US President
2013	Nelson Mandela dies at the age of 95
2013	Terrorist bombing at Boston marathon
2013	Edward Snowden leaks NSA documents and programs of espionage
2014	Ebola outbreaks in West Africa take the lives of 6,000
2014	Malaysia Airlines Flight 370 disappears
2014	ISIS Declares an Islamic Caliphate
2016	Britain Votes to Leave the European Union
2016	Donald Trump Wins the U.S. Presidency
2016	Fidel Castro dies at 90 years of age

Awards and Academia:
Rev. Sun Myung Moon and Dr. Hak Ja Han Moon

Rev. Sun Myung Moon

Honorary Doctorate of Law from Ricker College, USA (1975)

Honorary Doctorate of Law from La Plata University, Argentina (1984)

Honorary Doctorate of Divinity from Shaw Divinity School, USA (1985)

Honorary Doctorate of Humanities from Bridgeport University, USA (1995)

Honorary Doctorate of Literature from Sun Moon University (2002)

Awarded with the "Cross of Merit for Public Culture", Brazil (1986)

Awarded the Brazilian Cross of Merit for Public Culture and other decorations from other countries,1986

Awarded with the "Star of Freedom and Unification" by Organization for Integration in South America (1987)

Awarded with the highest decoration of the International Law Society, Mexico (1990)

Awarded with "Unification Award 1991" by International Unification Foundation, India (1991)

Awarded with the Universal Peace Award by General Assembly of IIFWP (2000)

Honorary Doctorate in Sacred Theology from Unification Theological Seminary, USA (2001)

Establishes the Holy Spirit Association for the Unification of World Christianity (HSA-UWC), 1954

Establishes the International Federation for Victory over Communism (IFVOC), 1968

Founds the Confederation of the Associations for the Unification of the Societies of the Americas (CAUSA), 1980

Establishes the Citizens' Federation for the Unification of the Fatherland (CFUF), Korea, 1987

Inaugurates the Summit Council for World Peace (1987)

Establishes the Inter-Religious Federation for World Peace (IRFWP), 1991

President of the Family Federation for World Peace and Unification (FFWPU), 1996

Establishes the Federation of Island Nations for World Peace, 1996

Establishes the Federation of Peninsular Nations for World Peace, 1996

Establishes the Federation of Continental Nations for World Peace, 1996

Establishes the Inter-religious and International Federation for World Peace (IIFWP), 1999

Establishes the Inter-religious International Peace Council (IIPC), 2003

Establishes Peace & Unity Family Party, Korea, 2003

Dr. Hak Ja Han Moon

While being the mother of 14 children and grandmother to over 40 grandchildren, Mrs. Moon receives the following awards and academic degrees:

Honorary Doctorate of Humanities from Bloomfield College, NJ, USA (1990)

Honorary Doctorate of Humanities from Bridgeport University, USA (1995)

Honorary Doctorate of Literature from Taiwan University of Culture (1999)

Honorary Doctorate of Pedagogics from Stefba Theological College of Bahia State, Brazil (1999)

Honorary Doctorate of Pedagogics from Kyrgyzstan State Pedagogical University (2000)

Honorary Doctorate of Philosophy from Upper Volga University, Russia (2000)

Honorary Doctorate of Humanities from Federico Enriquez Carbahal University, Dominical Republic (2000)

Honorary Doctorate in Sacred Theology from Unification Theological Seminary, USA (2001)

Awarded with the Grand Prix Peace Award of UN IAEWP (2001)

Honorary Doctorate of Literature from Sunmoon University (2002)

Career Achievements

President of the International Relief and Friendship Foundation(IRFF)

President of the Women's Federation for World Peace (WFWP)

President of Youth Federation for World Peace (YFWP)

President of Aewon, a volunteer organization

Co-President of Family Federation for World Peace and Unification (FFWPU), 1996

Co-founder of the Inter-religious and International Federation for World Peace ...(IIFWP)

President of Peace & Unity Family Party, Korea, 2003

Chairwoman of Cosmic True Parents Federation, 2000

Family Federation for a Heavenly USA

Copyright © HSA-UWC, 2018
The Holy Spirit Association for the Unification of Christianity
4 West 43rd Street, New York, NY 10036

First Printing 2018

All rights reserved. No part of this publication may be reproduced, stored in a retrieval system or transmitted in any form or by any means electronic, mechanical, photocopying, recording or otherwise without the prior written permission of the publisher.

ISBN 978-1-931166-85-0

Printed in the United States of America

www.ingramcontent.com/pod-product-compliance
Lightning Source LLC
Chambersburg PA
CBHW040200100526
44591CB00001B/3